Amy Schumer and Philosophy

Popular Culture and Philosophy® Series Editor: George A. Reisch

Volume 1 *Seinfeld and Philosophy: A Book about Everything and Nothing* (2000)

Volume 2 *The Simpsons and Philosophy: The D'oh! of Homer* (2001)

Volume 3 *The Matrix and Philosophy: Welcome to the Desert of the Real* (2002)

Volume 4 *Buffy the Vampire Slayer and Philosophy: Fear and Trembling in Sunnydale* (2003)

Volume 9 *Harry Potter and Philosophy: If Aristotle Ran Hogwarts* (2004)

Volume 12 *Star Wars and Philosophy: More Powerful than You Can Possibly Imagine* (2005)

Volume 13 *Superheroes and Philosophy: Truth, Justice, and the Socratic Way* (2005)

Volume 17 *Bob Dylan and Philosophy: It's Alright Ma (I'm Only Thinking)* (2006)

Volume 19 *Monty Python and Philosophy: Nudge Nudge, Think Think!* (2006)

Volume 30 *Pink Floyd and Philosophy: Careful with that Axiom, Eugene!* (2007)

Volume 35 *Star Trek and Philosophy: The Wrath of Kant* (2008)

Volume 36 *The Legend of Zelda and Philosophy: I Link Therefore I Am* (2008)

Volume 42 *Supervillains and Philosophy: Sometimes Evil Is Its Own Reward* (2009)

Volume 49 *Zombies, Vampires, and Philosophy: New Life for the Undead* (2010) Edited by Richard Greene and K. Silem Mohammad

Volume 54 *The Onion and Philosophy: Fake News Story True, Alleges Indignant Area Professor* (2010) Edited by Sharon M. Kaye

Volume 55 *Doctor Who and Philosophy: Bigger on the Inside* (2010) Edited by Courtland Lewis and Paula Smithka

Volume 57 *Rush and Philosophy: Heart and Mind United* (2010) Edited by Jim Berti and Durrell Bowman

Volume 58 *Dexter and Philosophy: Mind over Spatter* (2011) Edited by Richard Greene, George A. Reisch, and Rachel Robison-Greene

Volume 60 *SpongeBob SquarePants and Philosophy: Soaking Up Secrets Under the Sea!* (2011) Edited by Joseph J. Foy

Volume 61 *Sherlock Holmes and Philosophy: The Footprints of a Gigantic Mind* (2011) Edited by Josef Steiff

Volume 63 *Philip K. Dick and Philosophy: Do Androids Have Kindred Spirits?* (2011) Edited by D.E. Wittkower

Volume 64 *The Rolling Stones and Philosophy: It's Just a Thought Away* (2012) Edited by Luke Dick and George A. Reisch

Volume 67 *Breaking Bad and Philosophy: Badder Living through Chemistry* (2012) Edited by David R. Koepsell and Robert Arp

Volume 68 *The Walking Dead and Philosophy: Zombie Apocalypse Now* (2012) Edited by Wayne Yuen

Volume 69 *Curb Your Enthusiasm and Philosophy: Awaken the Social Assassin Within* (2012) Edited by Mark Ralkowski

Volume 74 *Planet of the Apes and Philosophy: Great Apes Think Alike* (2013) Edited by John Huss

Volume 75 *Psych and Philosophy: Some Dark Juju-Magumbo* (2013) Edited by Robert Arp

Volume 82 *Jurassic Park and Philosophy: The Truth Is Terrifying* (2014) Edited by Nicolas Michaud and Jessica Watkins

Volume 83 *The Devil and Philosophy: The Nature of His Game* (2014) Edited by Robert Arp

Volume 84 *Leonard Cohen and Philosophy: Various Positions* (2014) Edited by Jason Holt

Volume 85 *Homeland and Philosophy: For Your Minds Only* (2014) Edited by Robert Arp

Volume 86 *Girls and Philosophy: This Book Isn't a Metaphor for Anything* (2015) Edited by Richard Greene and Rachel Robison-Greene

Volume 87 *Adventure Time and Philosophy: The Handbook for Heroes* (2015) Edited by Nicolas Michaud

Volume 88 *Justified and Philosophy: Shoot First, Think Later* (2015) Edited by Rod Carveth and Robert Arp

Volume 89 *Steve Jobs and Philosophy: For Those Who Think Different* (2015) Edited by Shawn E. Klein

Volume 90 *Dracula and Philosophy: Dying to Know* (2015) Edited by Nicolas Michaud and Janelle Pötzsch

Volume 91 *It's Always Sunny and Philosophy: The Gang Gets Analyzed* (2015) Edited by Roger Hunt and Robert Arp

Volume 92 *Orange Is the New Black and Philosophy: Last Exit from Litchfield* (2015) Edited by Richard Greene and Rachel Robison-Greene

Volume 93 *More Doctor Who and Philosophy: Regeneration Time* (2015) Edited by Courtland Lewis and Paula Smithka

Volume 94 *Divergent and Philosophy: The Factions of Life* (2016) Edited by Courtland Lewis

Volume 95 *Downton Abbey and Philosophy: Thinking in That Manor* (2016) Edited by Adam Barkman and Robert Arp

Volume 96 *Hannibal Lecter and Philosophy: The Heart of the Matter* (2016) Edited by Joseph Westfall

Volume 97 *The Ultimate Walking Dead and Philosophy: Hungry for More* (2016) Edited by Wayne Yuen

Volume 98 *The Princess Bride and Philosophy: Inconceivable!* (2016) Edited by Richard Greene and Rachel Robison-Greene

Volume 99 *Louis C.K. and Philosophy: You Don't Get to Be Bored* (2016) Edited by Mark Ralkowski

Volume 100 *Batman, Superman, and Philosophy: Badass or Boyscout?* (2016) Edited by Nicolas Michaud

Volume 101 *Discworld and Philosophy: Reality Is Not What It Seems* (2016) Edited by Nicolas Michaud

Volume 102 *Orphan Black and Philosophy: Grand Theft DNA* (2016) Edited by Richard Greene and Rachel Robison-Greene

Volume 103 *David Bowie and Philosophy: Rebel Rebel* (2016) Edited by Theodore G. Ammon

Volume 104 *Red Rising and Philosophy: Break the Chains!* (2016) Edited by Courtland Lewis and Kevin McCain

Volume 105 *The Ultimate Game of Thrones and Philosophy: You Think or Die* (2017) Edited by Eric J. Silverman and Robert Arp

Volume 106 *Peanuts and Philosophy: You're a Wise Man, Charlie Brown!* (2017) Edited by Richard Greene and Rachel Robison-Greene

Volume 107 *Deadpool and Philosophy: My Common Sense Is Tingling* (2017) Edited by Nicolas Michaud

Volume 108 *The X-Files and Philosophy: The Truth Is In Here* (2017) Edited by Robert Arp

Volume 109 *Mr. Robot and Philosophy: Beyond Good and Evil Corp.* (2017) Edited by Richard Greene and Rachel Robison-Greene

Volume 110 *Hamilton and Philosophy: Revolutionary Thinking* (2017) Edited by Aaron Rabinowitz and Robert Arp

Volume 111 *The Man in the High Castle and Philosophy: Subversive Reports from Another Reality* (2017) Edited by Bruce Krajewski and Joshua Heter

Volume 112 *The Americans and Philosophy: Reds in the Bed* (2018) Edited by Robert Arp and Kevin Guilfoy

Volume 113 *Jimi Hendrix and Philosophy: Experience Required* (2018) Edited by Theodore G. Ammon

Volume 114 *American Horror Story and Philosophy: Life Is But a Nightmare* (2018) Edited by Richard Greene and Rachel Robison-Greene

Volume 115 *Iron Man vs. Captain America and Philosophy* (2018) Edited by Nicolas Michaud and Jessica Watkins

Volume 116 *1984 and Philosophy: Is Resistance Futile?* (2018) Edited by Ezio Di Nucci and Stefan Storrie

Volume 117 *The Dark Tower and Philosophy* (2018) Edited by Nicolas Michaud and Jacob Thomas May

Volume 118 *Scott Adams and Philosophy: A Hole in the Fabric of Reality* (2018) Edited by Daniel Yim, Galen Foresman, and Robert Arp

Volume 119 *Twin Peaks and Philosophy: That's Damn Fine Philosophy!* (2018) Edited by Richard Greene and Rachel Robison-Greene

Volume 120 *Amy Schumer and Philosophy: Brainwreck!* (2018) Edited by Charlene Elsby and Rob Luzecky

Titles in Preparation:

The Twilight Zone and Philosophy (2018) Edited by Heather L. Rivera amd Alexander E. Hooke

Westworld and Philosophy (2018) Edited by Richard Greene and Joshua Heter

The Handmaid's Tale and Philosophy (2018) Edited by Rachel Robison-Greene

Rick and Morty and Philosophy (2018) Edited by Lester C. Abesamis and Wayne Yuen

Tom Petty and Philosophy (2018) Edited by Randall E. Auxier and Megan Volpert

Stranger Things and Philosophy (2019) Edited by Jeffey A. Ewing and Andrew M. Winters

For full details of all Popular Culture and Philosophy® books, visit www.opencourtbooks.com.

Popular Culture and Philosophy®

Amy Schumer and Philosophy

Brainwreck!

EDITED BY

Charlene Elsby and
Rob Luzecky

OPEN COURT
Chicago

Volume 120 in the series, Popular Culture and Philosophy®, edited by George A. Reisch

To find out more about Open Court books, visit our website at www.opencourtbooks.com.

Open Court Publishing Company is a division of Carus Publishing Company, dba Cricket Media.

First printing 2018

Printed and bound in the United States of America.

Amy Schumer and Philosophy: Brainwreck!

ISBN: 978-0-8126-9990-6

This book is also available as an e-book.

Library of Congress Cataloging-in-Publication Data
Names: Elsby, Charlene, editor. | Luzecky, Rob, 1974- editor.
Title: Amy Schumer and philosophy / edited by Charlene Elsby and Rob Luzecky.
Description: Chicago : Open Court, [2018] | Series: Popular culture and philosophy ; volume 120
Identifiers: LCCN 2018003765 | ISBN 9780812699906 (trade paper : alk. paper)
Subjects: LCSH: Schumer, Amy—Criticism and interpretation. | Popular culture—Philosophy.
Classification: LCC PN2287.S3365 A49 2018 | DDC 792.702/8092—dc23
LC record available at https://lccn.loc.gov/2018003765

Contents

Dear Amy

CHARLENE ELSBY

I hope that you don't mind that we put together this book about you. You see, as philosophers, we like to take the things we love and then analyze the shit out of them. We like to take things apart, divide them up into tiny logical pieces, then play with them like Legos, making combinations and comparisons, anything we can do within the limits of plausible interpretation. Then we die, and (hopefully) someone else does the same thing to us. Most of the time, the people we talk about are dead people—specifically, white men—who aren't going to post on the internet about how dickish we are for doing such things. (The discipline definitely has a diversity problem; we're trying to do something about that.)

Popular Culture and Philosophy books are a trick we use to make people who like things and stuff pay attention to philosophy as well. We take something people like, and we write about it, because we like it too. But also, we think that maybe once your fans are done watching your show, memorizing your movie scripts, poring over your book and scouring the internet for interviews, they might pick up our book. Then the happy feelings they have about you will leak over to philosophy itself, and then they might care when the powers that be come and decide we're bad for the public good. (It happens every few years. Don't worry, though; we've been around for a while now, and while every so often someone gets executed for corrupting the youth, somehow we always seem to get by.) A lot of the time, these Popular Culture and Philosophy books are about a show, or a movie, or a bunch of movies, but I wanted to make this one about you, because you're great, and you do so many things.

This is where it all started. In 2016, I demanded my sister buy me your book for my birthday, and I went with her to the store to get it, just to make sure she got the right one. I watched most of your sketches on YouTube, because I was in Canada at the time, and Hulu hates Canada and everyone in it. When I finished *The Girl with the Lower Back Tattoo*, I came up with a new life plan and posted it to Facebook. Twenty three people liked it.

Charlene Elsby
August 27, 2016 ·

New life plan: I propose a volume on Amy Schumer and Philosophy; she reads about it and is all like, "Fuck that shit." But then she realizes I'm actually pretty awesome, and we hang out when I'm in New York or she's in Indiana.

So far, it's going pretty well. I proposed the book to Open Court, and they liked the idea. It's the first Popular Culture and Philosophy volume I've edited, but I've written a lot of things for them in the past, so I pretty much know what I'm doing here. I usually work on these things with my husband (co-editor Rob Luzecky), and he was on board immediately. He likes things that are great, just like I do. Plus, he does half of the work, while everyone just assumes that I'm the *real* Amy Schumer fan.

A nice thing about this book is that when I mention it, people automatically start comparing me to you. A couple of months ago, I listed you as a research interest at a job interview (because of this book), and one of the professors judging me approached me afterward, to tell me that she could now see that we're basically the same person. I like to encourage these comparisons. Rob stopped me from including a picture here of our faces morphed together. He says it's creepy. Like I would ever really try to mash our pixels together to form one amazing face of greatness. (I wouldn't; the technology doesn't exist.) I didn't get the job.

I also have a lower back tattoo. It's a sun, moon, and star design that I drew myself when I was sixteen and awesome. You have a sister who's awesome, while my sister is also awesome. Plus, Rob says that I look like you in that picture we used to solicit papers for this book. So you see, we're basically the same. At the same time, I don't *really* expect us to become best friends. We're both introverted, except where all of our life choices are concerned, so we'd have to have a buffer to make it not terribly awkward. Or perhaps we could work out a conversation in advance, and then do that several times over several years, until we're used to one another and you forget that we're friends because I took it upon myself to dissect your work and convince a bunch of other philosophers to do the same thing.

It must be weird to meet people who think they already know everything about you. I probably don't even know *that* much, but I do think that paying attention to everything you do and then putting together this book about you has so far made our relationship pretty one-sided. I tell Rob that you're my Bradley Cooper—or were my Bradley Cooper, before Bradley Cooper decided to write and direct that movie remake where we're all supposed to think he's such a great guy for being willing to pity fuck Lady Gaga. It's Lady Fucking Gaga, for fuck's sake. It's not like she's Rosario Dawson. (Yes, we've all heard the story about how Lady Gaga wasn't seen as a pop star by the music industry for a little while when she was getting started. I think we're all agreed now that the music industry was wrong and stupid on that one. Keep up, *Brad.*)

When I posted my new life plan to Facebook, one of my former students commented that you were often in Chicago, which is only about three hours away from Fort Wayne, Indiana. I've been to Chicago at least five times now, but I haven't run into you yet. One of these times, perhaps I'll see you on the street and (after asking politely), we could take a selfie that I then couldn't post on the internet because my face looks weird (and I don't want to ask you to take five more until it looks right).

I figure that you probably have someone in charge of reading things that come out about you. I figure that person will be reading this book, and I hope that they say, "What a nice book. The people who did it are good people." I'm not trying to tell you how to do your job, but maybe after you read this little introduction, you'll actually think that, and if that's what you think, well, that's one grammatically correct way to say it to Amy.

I

Persona Non Grata

1
Amy's Self-Confidence and Self-Deprecation

CAMILLE ATKINSON

Amy Schumer's self-deprecating humor is a brilliantly skillful means of overcoming shame. She acknowledges this herself in the concluding chapter of *The Girl with the Lower Back Tattoo*: "I had to learn (I'm still learning) how to choose to be proud of who I am rather than ashamed" (pp. 312–13).

Instead of allowing herself to be shamed by others, or to suffer embarrassment over the imperfections that make her an individual, she embraces, rises above, and accepts them. However, what she doesn't seem to recognize is the extent to which she inspires or reminds others (especially women) that they too can find relief in humor and, ironically, self-confidence in self-deprecation.

It's no secret that Schumer frequently earns praise for her courage, clear-eyed honesty, and a ready willingness to take on tough topics. However, she doesn't get nearly enough credit for standing out as a uniquely inspiring comedian. So, what makes her so one-of-a-kind? I believe the answer lies in the content of her material, as well as in how she approaches it.

A less than "perfect" body, blackout drinking, binge eating, and "grape"—as in, "gray area rape" or non-consensual sex—along with the myriad ways in which family and friends break our hearts or let us down, are sources of pain and insecurity for many, but most especially for women.

Rather than hiding her flaws and failures, denying her suffering or wallowing in shame, Schumer faces life's unpleasant realities directly and fearlessly. She's among the very few comics to be so consistently and relentlessly self-deprecating and, at the same time, exuding confidence. She is not only laughing at herself but openly and generously encouraging her audience to laugh along with her and, hopefully, at themselves as well. This makes it possible for her to connect more intimately with her audiences, and it paves the way for a deeper kind of acceptance.

On the other hand, Schumer's self-deprecation is not always taken as ironically as she intends and, sometimes, her honesty seems brutal. On other occasions, she appears to be playing into female stereotypes, even reinforcing them, as opposed to questioning or critiquing them. Finally, in some cases, the crudeness of the content overwhelms the humor, and she is blamed for demeaning herself or women in general.

Most of the time, such criticisms not only miss the joke, they miss the point. Certainly, some of her jokes are cringe-inducing or awkward, while others bomb resoundingly. Still, Schumer's satirical stance not only allows her to personally transcend cultural prejudices (regarding the impossible ideal body types imposed on women, what constitutes socially acceptable female behavior, how to deal with less-than-perfect loved ones, and so forth), she invites others to share in the joke and reflect on their own flaws, insecurities, and expectations.

Her TV sketches, stand-up routines, movies, and writing are not exercises in humiliation, either hers or women's in general, but hilariously funny demonstrations of a character trait that's all too rare in the twenty-first century—namely, humility. Schumer's humor is quintessentially feminist in nature, generous in spirit, personally liberating, socially important and politically significant. This is possible because she invites women as well as men to laugh *at and with* her.

So, what are the essential ingredients that allow her jokes to land so delightfully, and what is missing when they don't?

Transcendence, Connection, Acceptance

When Schumer's self-deprecation succeeds, it is due to the fact that her jokes open up a space for transcendence, connection, and acceptance.

- *Transcendence* takes place when one rises above difficult circumstances by laughing at or making light of them. To joke about a deeply painful but unavoidable situation enables one to detach from or overcome it. For instance, if I can laugh at my mistakes, hurt feelings, or the absurd realities of human existence, I can bear them more easily and move on more quickly.
- *Connection* happens when you establish intimacy with another person or persons, and jokes can be a shortcut to this kind of interpersonal identification. For instance, if someone appreciates or laughs at my joke, it means we have something in common, which may inspire us to overlook our differences, forgive our foibles, and get to know one other better. Thus, humor is something that makes community possible or reinforces social cohesion.

These two elements, transcendence and connection, are essential for self-deprecation to be successful. However, there is also a third element, acceptance, which is a sort of bonus.

- *Acceptance* is a deeper form of transcendence, insofar as it involves the kind of overcoming that occurs when we finally make peace with or come to terms with an inevitable, heartbreaking reality—for example, that someone I love can't love me the way I want to be loved, that hard work doesn't always pay off or lead to a successful career, and so forth.

You can come to a place of acceptance in solitude, or in the company of others, but it is not possible to get there without the assistance of others. I may be said to have reached a point of acceptance when I am not only able to acknowledge but to personally *integrate*, perhaps even embrace, a particularly painful part of my life (divorce), or one of the cruel ironies of human existence (death). However, the acceptance of realities like these is only possible after some personal transcendence and communion with others has taken place.

The humorous confrontation of the absurd, yet all-too-real aspects of the human condition, is why Schumer's work has been so successful, and why she has such a devoted fan base. Listening to her jokes, watching her in action, or simply reading about her life experiences, makes us feel less alone. In sum, by playfully inviting us to laugh *at* as well as *with* her, Schumer makes it at least a little bit easier to accept life's disappointments and one's own failures.

I don't mean to say that all of Schumer's jokes successfully meet these criteria. I found some aspects of *Snatched* to be rather disappointing, on precisely these grounds. While *Trainwreck* also relied on self-deprecation, it depicted scenarios with which most could identify—such as fear of commitment or dealing with the death of a loved one.

Snatched begins similarly, with scenes emphasizing the lead character's shallowness or self-centeredness, but soon it detours into crude situations that I wish were relatable but instead come off as ludicrously bizarre. And the most *un*-funny scenes lean more towards degradation or humiliation than transcendence and acceptance.

So, if Schumer's brand of self-deprecation is successful because she's *not* shaming herself and other women, but seeking to empower, when and why do these other joke-efforts miss the mark? How and when do her attempts at humor manage to express a healthy *humility* instead of hurtful or hyperbolic *humiliation*? Schumer herself admits that, even when she's the target of a joke, her ultimate objective is to overcome and to move beyond the pain, and to encourage others to do likewise. On page 56 of *The Girl with the Lower Back Tattoo*, she says, "I look at the saddest things in life and laugh at how awful they are, because they are hilarious and it's all we can do with moments that are painful." And on page 139, she says, "I write about things that I'm truly sensitive about, and I'm often the butt of the joke." Thus, whether a joke kills or bombs, her goal is noteworthy and noble. So, how to distinguish between the jokes, or attempts at humor, that are humiliating and those which promote transcendence, connection, and acceptance?

Self-Deprecation and Gallows Humor

According to Sigmund Freud, humor and laughter are pleasurable because they relieve tension. Laughing at a joke or seeking the humor in an uncomfortable or unpleasant situation releases the kind of energy that would otherwise be used to contain or repress feelings. Usually, these are the kinds of feelings that are deemed socially unacceptable or that we are discouraged from publicly expressing—anger, shame, sexual desire, and grief.

"Gallows humor" is the kind of humor that treats serious or painful subject matter in a lighthearted or ironic way. Making light of terminal illness or death represent the most obvious cases, hence the term "gallows," but making fun of terrifying situations, rejection or heartbreak, broken dreams, and other disappointing aspects of life, illustrates this attitude just as well. Moreover, Schumer herself embraces this darker perspective or "twisted" sense of humor, making liberal use of it in her own work. In her memoir, some of the funniest *and* most poignant instances of this genre involve her father's struggle with MS (multiple sclerosis), and nonconsensual sex ("grape"). On page 90, she advises, "I hope all parents talk to their kids about consent and, when you do, please, please don't make the mistake my mother made. Don't do it over a bowl of clam chowder."

Amy Schumer is capable of being deadly serious when discussing tragedies in general (not just her own or those of her family members). When she confronts the deaths of two women killed during a screening of *Trainwreck*, she makes no apologies for devoting an entire chapter to the problem of gun violence. On page 277, she briefly digresses and assumes the role of a heckling reader, "*Get back to telling us your vagina jokes! Make us laugh, clown!*" However, it is abundantly clear that she is *not* making light of the loss or incident itself. She is neither having a laugh at someone else's expense nor minimizing what happened. Instead, Schumer is allowing herself to be vulnerable in a way we don't expect, sharing her grief, and acknowledging that her message here is as personal as it is political. Still, whether she's striking a serious tone, employing self-deprecation, using gallows humor or ironic hyperbole, Schumer is offering her readers and viewers a front-row seat to her pain and personal transcendence. From this metaphorical or literal seat, we witness her troubles and how she overcomes them. She provides a means of connection.

Self-deprecation and gallows humor have a lot in common. Both types of humor largely depend on context and are often misunderstood. Like self-deprecating humor, which is often taken literally or regarded as evidence of low self-worth, jokes that are dark or macabre tend to invite criticism or are interpreted as indicating a lack of sensitivity and compassion. In either case, missing the spirit and intention of Schumer's humor is a mistake.

Even though many folks may not have a taste for gallows humor, its objective is to provide relief—relief from the kind of searing pain that would not even be felt if one were not already sensitized to the hurt of others. Thus, the emphasis here is on one's connectedness to other human beings. Similarly, when Schumer's self-deprecating jokes work, it is because they show how accepting she is of herself and her own limitations, indicating a stronger, more profound sense of self-worth than what appears on the surface. Given that both self-deprecation and gallows humor are so deeply rooted in irony, it is no wonder that such jokes, and the comics who rely so heavily on them, are so frequently misinterpreted.

So, how to determine which jokes fit the relief model of humor, and which don't? I believe Schumer's jokes—whether dark or light, self-deprecating or satirical—are most effective when she connects with others by modeling transcendence or acceptance. The most successful jokes are those that show

how she has found her way forward, establish a uniquely human connection, and demonstrate what it means to accept fundamental absurdities of the human condition. By laughing at herself and inviting others to laugh along with her, she helps her audience feel more connected to each other, to overcome or, at least, overlook our own failures, and accept life's otherwise unacceptable realities. And, as paradoxical as it might sound, this talent for self-deprecation and gallows humor is as much of an indication of Schumer's hard-earned self-confidence as it is of her compassion and humility.

Humility and Humiliation

Humor has its roots in humility, not the humiliation of oneself or anyone else. This is because it requires the kind of self-reflection that enables us to learn how to live with (even celebrate) human imperfection in oneself and others. Every adult person, at some point in his or her life, has faced one or more unpleasant realities that force us to choose between *fighting* ourselves or *laughing* at ourselves. Moreover, any time we can get others to laugh along with us by making fun of ourselves, we do more than merely transcend our own insecurities, foibles, or disappointment—we find our way to acceptance.

In this respect, self-deprecation succeeds or fails in ways similar to that of gallows humor. What, for example, could be more painful than witnessing the suffering of a beloved parent or being "graped" by a boyfriend? And, what could be more embarrassing than blackout drinking, an awkward one-night stand, or secret binge-eating? But, most significantly, what better place to find comfort than among those who can understand or identify with these absurd realities, and laugh at them? By making fun of her own pain, misadventures, and imperfections, Schumer models what it means to be confidently humble or humbly confident. As she puts it on page 237, "It's relaxing sometimes just being human."

This is the kind of humility that consists in the fundamental acceptance of one's powerlessness or limitations. We accept life's unavoidable absurdities in a world that, in one way or another, "breaks all of us" (to quote Hemingway). Or, as my father put it, "sooner or later, life sandpapers everybody's ass." It is human *hubris* or pride that insists otherwise, creating a space not for comedy but tragedy. It wasn't just Hamlet's *hubris* that convinced him he could avenge his father's death, or the pride of Oedipus that told him he was superior to his fate, or even Schumer's mother's "projected flawlessness and innocence" (described on page 236), which seems to have prevented her from putting her children's needs ahead of her own. On the contrary, everyone denies their humanity in one way or another, pretends to be something they are not, or is blind to their own selfishness. Heroic efforts to transcend the human condition or to fix others are, for the most part, just a means of avoiding ourselves—of focusing on what is wrong in one's environment rather than on what is broken in oneself.

We all have duties to others, to community or country, family or friends, and so forth. However, anytime we head off on a crusade against injustice, give advice to a loved one, or attempt to solve someone else's problems, without considering our own capacities or limitations, there is not only room for error but the very real chance of making things worse. As my dad has so often reminded me, "Kid, you're so right, you're wrong!" That is to say, self-righteousness or blind faith in oneself can create a hell all its own.

Referring to her mother and how she was raised, Schumer acknowledges this too: "I still wish she could have just been honest with us. And with herself. We're all trying our best, making mistakes, and hanging on by a thread . . . I wish my mother understood this too." (p. 237) Simply put, why not celebrate failure as much as success? Perhaps Schumer's comedy is inspired by her mother's own example of how *not* to be in this world? Either way, the valuable service Schumer provides is to make herself the butt of the joke, maintaining both her confidence and sanity, and inviting others to join in with her.

When the Jokes Don't Work

It's precisely Schumer's deadpan acceptance of who she is that is so inspiring. The humor is in her humility and the invitation extended to each audience member to laugh and do likewise. Instead of exacerbating a painful situation by trying to hide her emotional needs or personal foibles, Schumer calls attention to them. And this is as true of her physical comedy as it is of her jokes or stand-up. Being able to laugh not only provides psychological relief, it can also be a way of taking responsibility for oneself without wallowing in shame or humiliation.

When Schumer's jokes or attempts at humor don't work, it's usually due to a couple of missing elements. First, some of the failed jokes or humorous situations are simply unique to her or her character's life experience, which makes it difficult, if not impossible, for a general audience to identify with them. Second, some scenarios seem geared more towards humiliation than humility, which is more likely to generate disgust than the laughter of relief, connection, or acceptance.

Early scenes in *Snatched* had me laughing and nodding my head in agreement. This was because Schumer's character, Emily, displayed vulnerability and revealed some of the not-so-flattering human characteristics typical of Schumer's comedy. Some of the most hilarious scenes were when Emily was obtusely oblivious as her boyfriend tries to break up with her, mindlessly chattering about the vacation she's preparing for instead of assisting a customer in the workplace, or competing for her mother's attention with her brother.

None of these traits is particularly unusual or unique to the character. Rather, they are all common to human beings in general, making them easy to identify with and to laugh at. What adult person hasn't been in denial when confronted with rejection from a close friend or lover? Who hasn't been embarrassed by his or her own egocentrism at one time or another? And certainly, there is nothing new or novel about sibling rivalry. These distinctly human flaws are something anyone can relate to, or *should* be able to identify with. We recognize ourselves in Emily's character and find a sense of solidarity and community.

On the other hand, the tapeworm scene in *Snatched* is as bizarre as it is unrealistic, as tapeworms can't be lured out of someone's mouth by a piece of meat. The other scene that left me cold was the one in which Emily flirts with the man who is both her love interest and responsible for her and her mother being "snatched" in the first place. These attempts at humor fail, because they leave Emily degraded or humiliated rather than empowered. In other words, they illustrate a female character being undone or overwhelmed by her circumstances, not overcoming or transcending them.

Contracting a parasite is nothing to be ashamed of, but there is nothing to overcome—it's merely a physical ailment to be cured. And there's little in the tapeworm incident that would bring people together or inspire us to embrace a common humanity. Simply put, the tapeworm scene misses the mark by being so grossly exaggerated and crudely unrealistic that there is nothing with which others might identify or connect. In sum, it evokes more discomfort and disgust than it does appreciation for silly self-deprecation, much less a recognition of what it means to be imperfectly human in any meaningful way.

The flirting scene fails primarily because the timing and context are off. To be sure, there are precious few grown women (and men) who can't relate to being attracted to someone of dubious character. However, it's not as if Emily is suffering from a case of Stockholm Syndrome or has been a victim of domestic abuse. Rather, the interest Emily shows is completely out of place. At best, this scene is gratuitous in a way that is difficult, if not impossible, to identify or connect with; at worst, it makes her character appear either dysfunctionally desperate or astonishingly stupid, or both.

And When They Do

Compare this to Schumer's use of self-deprecation in *The Girl with the Lower Back Tattoo*, when she describes a brief rendezvous with an ex-boyfriend who had been abusive: "we got back together one more time . . . during the New York City blackout of 2003. (In that heat, I would have fucked a salamander)" (p. 183). In this case, Schumer's self-deprecating humor demonstrates the kind of resilience that others can relate to or be inspired by. After all, what self-reflective adult (male or female) hasn't regretted at least *one* choice in relation to a lover or ex-lover, made in the heat of the moment?

By contrast, the flirtation scene in *Snatched* makes Emily herself the butt of the joke, not by overcoming sexist stereotypes or by taking responsibility for her misplaced feelings and laughing at them, but simply by succumbing to them. Thus, even if some viewers do find it funny, they are laughing *at* Emily rather than *with* her. In sum, this scene is not an illustration of humorous self-deprecation and transcendence but of humiliating self-degradation and effacement.

Schumer's first movie, *Trainwreck,* could be described as one, long self-deprecating joke. For virtually the entire film, Schumer's character (also named Amy), reveals herself to be both a "deeply sexual being" and a "commitment-phobe." This results in several funny scenes in which she challenges traditional views of women and sex, underscoring this point in her memoir (on page 266): *Trainwreck* was "a story about a woman from the woman's point of view." It was about "equal opportunity."

Trainwreck was equally prolific in its depiction of gallows humor which, in most cases, involves the use of self-deprecation as well. For instance, Emily becomes verbally abusive towards her boyfriend, Aaron, following her father's funeral. Audience members, like me, who can relate, found themselves laughing with outlandish delight as well as squirming in discomfort. I too have been guilty of bad behavior due to grief over the loss of a loved one! This scene was particularly memorable, because it allowed me to feel a little less ashamed, a little less alone, and a lot more human.

Schumer's jokes succeed first when they show her or one of her characters overcoming a personal disappointment or failure—her father's alcoholism and debilitating illness, her mother's infidelity and fall from grace, being stuck in an abusive relationship or being a perfectly imperfect human. Schumer provides a wonderful model for how others, particularly women, might transcend these challenges, because she so often seamlessly connects with her audience on a deeper level. By skillfully modeling an ironic approach to self-esteem, by making us laugh both *at* and *with* her, we see how and why Amy Schumer's self-deprecating humor is worth emulating.

Schumer's jokes allow her to connect with the audience, because she makes fun of failure. She finds the *fun* in failure, rather than being victimized or undone by it. Whenever Amy jokes about herself, she invites each of us to look at our own lives or imperfections in a lighthearted manner, even when we can't relate to or identify with the details. Whether or not I too am "Mrs. Potato Head" shaped or, as an infant, "resembled a pug more than a baby" (as Schumer describes herself on pages 217 and 118, respectively), I can always laugh at the hyperbole and connect with the feeling of being less-than-attractive at one time or another.

Schumer's jokes inspire both her *and* her audience to embrace their own foibles and to resign themselves to the myriad absurdities of living a human life. This element of acceptance is what makes her humor so appealing across sex or gender boundaries. Because Schumer is so skillful at modeling what one might call an "extreme acceptance" of herself, her humor can be appreciated by men and women alike.

Schumer's humor has a great effect. Not only is it intelligent and cathartic, providing comfort as well as food for thought, it's also a clever means for empowering women both personally and politically, inspiring us to forgive ourselves, and cultivating a more hilarious understanding of the relationship between the sexes.

2
"Brave"

DANIEL MALLOY

Much of Amy Schumer's comedy is self-deprecating, and it plays on popular perceptions of both herself and women more generally. A fair number of her jokes attempt to have fun with and slyly subvert behaviors and attitudes justly characterized as "shaming."

Such behaviors and attitudes richly deserve to be ridiculed and undermined as often as possible. But it's not clear that self-deprecating jokes based on shaming actually achieve that goal. What is the object of ridicule in such jokes? Is it the shaming attitudes, or the person telling the joke? In the first case, such jokes undermine shaming, but in the second, self-deprecating jokes only serve to reinforce such attitudes.

If self-deprecating jokes involve ridiculing the joke teller, then I'd say that they reinforce shaming instead of discouraging it. We should have legitimate concerns about self-deprecating humor. It is not always good or funny to go around cutting yourself down for a laugh. On the other hand, a self-deprecating joke done right, as Schumer's are, protects the joke teller and successfully ridicules whatever standard it's based on—in this case, a standard that supports shaming. Schumer's comedy is self-deprecation done right.

I Think I'm, Like, So Pretty

Let's be good philosophers and try to clarify exactly what we're talking about. You deprecate yourself when you intentionally and knowingly underrate your value or contribution. That should get us started. Self-deprecation is closely linked to humility and modesty and their evil doubles, false humility and false modesty. What differentiates it from these virtues and vices is twofold.

First, humility and modesty and their false doubles describe patterns of behavior or habits. Self-deprecation, while it may be a habit, need not be. It's more often dealt with as an individual action. The second distinction has to do with the attitudes and assessments involved in each of these concepts. You are genuinely humble or modest if you have a fair assessment of your own value—you simply seek proper recognition for others or recognition for yourself that is justified by your value. The falsely modest or falsely humble, on the other hand, tend to overestimate their value or contribution, and engage in their antics in order to get others to agree with them.

Humility and modesty need not even describe patterns of behavior. They can just describe your attitude toward yourself. Self-deprecation, on the other hand, while it embodies an attitude, is more than just an attitude. Self-deprecation, like false modesty or false humility, must be expressed. Just as false modesty and false humility are invitations to others to correct their supposed misapprehension of your value, self-deprecation is an invitation to others to ignore or degrade your value.

So far, self-deprecation sounds awful. It seems that going around saying to everyone that you suck at life is not a great way to live, and really not a good way to express yourself. The self-deprecator may deserve pity, though they are unlikely to get it. But we don't always think of self-deprecation this way. That's because, most often, self-deprecation is understood humorously. "Serious self-deprecation" isn't a contradiction in terms, though it may be cause for concern. Such a person would see no value in themselves or their contributions.

Somehow, the addition of humor can provide a kind of shield for the self-deprecator. Making a self-deprecating comment in a humorous way reassures us that some element of the comment is false, or at least not believed by the self-deprecator. That gives us permission to join the self-deprecator in their self-deprecation without worrying that we will demean or degrade them.

Humor renders self-deprecation safe, for both the self-deprecator and their audience. The question then becomes: Why? The answer to that question is tied to which aspect of the self-deprecating act we're not meant to take seriously.

Reality Shows Make Me Feel So Much Better about Myself

Philosophers traditionally haven't spent a great deal of time or effort puzzling out the mysteries of humor. We've been busy trying to fathom the mysteries of existence, like "Is there a God?" and "How do I make a living as a philosopher?" But a few have been looking at what makes us laugh, and they've come up with a few possible answers. One possible answer is found in superiority theory. According to this theory, what makes us laugh is a positive comparison between ourselves and the butt of the joke. That is, when I laugh, it's because I perceive that I'm better than whatever or whomever I'm laughing at. Superiority theory maintains that there is no laughter without a butt—someone or something to laugh at. Laughter, then, always has an element of cruelty about it. According to superiority theory, when someone laughs at you, they are the sort of dickhead that thinks that they are better than you.

So, for superiority theory, it's easy to see why self-deprecation can be humorous. When Schumer tells us, "I'm the worst dancer. I dance like your aunt at a wedding. Like every move that I do, I'm surprising myself" (*Mostly Sex Stuff*), she makes herself the butt of the joke, and invites us to feel superior to her. And hence, we laugh. Not with her, but at her, or at least at her professed inability to dance well.

This may seem pretty benign, but think about some of Schumer's more representative jokes. As she's noted, she's considered a sex comic, because a large part of her act deals with her sex life. But no joke exists in a vacuum, including sex jokes. So, when Schumer says "I've only been with four people. That was a weird night" (*Mostly Sex Stuff*), she's eliciting laughter from us, because we haven't had such weird nights. But also because (according to some of the more puritanical people in the audience, that is to say, most of us) there is something wrong or off about people who do have such "weird" nights. By making light of the behavior, she confirms the standard that condemns it. Schumer's self-deprecation thus seems to play into and support slut-shaming. Every joke is a judgment against the butt of the joke, but also a reaffirmation of the standard the butt violated. This standard is the basis for slut-shaming, which the joke, by extension, encourages.

So, when Amy jokes that, "I've never said this sentence in my life: I forgot to have lunch today" (*Live at the Apollo*), she validates the idea that as a woman, she should match a certain body-type—one maintained by people who forget about meals. Further, she makes it safe for her audience (us) to maintain that ideal. We maintain that ideal by body-shaming women, including Schumer herself. According to the implicit morality of Amy Schumer's jokes, women should be thin and dainty, sober and chaste, quiet and passive; and any woman who isn't all of these things is a legitimate target of ridicule and shame.

A Lot of These Are Jokes

Every joke covered by superiority theory affirms some value or standard by pointing out how the butt of the joke fails to live up to it. What makes self-deprecating jokes unique is the fact that the joke-teller is also the butt of the joke. The self-deprecator could just as easily and accurately be labeled a self-shamer. This combination creates an interesting ethical challenge, because it means that the joke-teller is both judge and defendant, the one offering the condemnation and the condemned.

This may not seem to be much of a problem, and it often isn't. Acknowledging our shortcomings is how we learn and grow and get better. So there's nothing inherently problematic about self-deprecating humor. But there are two scenarios where self-deprecating jokes become cause for concern. The first is when they are excessive. It's one thing for a person to humorously acknowledge a particular flaw or set of flaws when the occasion arises. We all do that. Some of us make jokes about our bad handwriting (guilty!) or how we're bad at math. But there are some self-deprecators who can't wait for the occasion to arise. They don't limit their jokes to one or two areas that need improvement. They are awful at everything. This kind of self-deprecator utterly lacks self-respect. Their jokes take the sting out of the rejection they not only expect, but also believe they deserve. They're not looking for laughs; they're inviting shame.

Plainly, Amy Schumer isn't this sort of self-deprecator. If we just go by her stand-up specials, some of the most self-deprecating jokes are qualified by caveats reminding us that either these are just jokes or that Amy doesn't have self-esteem problems. At one point, she reassures the audience, "Don't feel bad for me. I think I'm, like, so pretty" (*Live at Gotham*). Amy's self-deprecation shouldn't make us worry about her. If it did, it wouldn't be funny. As fellow comedian Marc Maron once observed about his own sets, about half the audience leaves saying, "That was so fucking funny"; the other half leaves saying, "I hope he's okay" (Marc Maron, *Final Engagement*). You leave a Schumer set assured that she's okay.

No, the cause for concern in Schumer's self-deprecating humor isn't its degree, but its basis. Schumer's jokes at her own expense espouse a certain set of values, and those values are the problem. Think of it like this: when we make self-deprecating jokes, it's usually about some generally harmless flaw. Having bad handwriting may be annoying, but it generally doesn't do any damage.

But Amy Schumer's self-deprecating jokes aren't harmless. The values they espouse are harmful, or at least potentially so. The most common values advocated by Amy's self-deprecation are chastity, sobriety, and thinness. There's nothing inherently harmful about any of these values, but seeing someone who is or seems to be moderate about each deprecate herself for being excessive makes the advocacy harmful. A healthy woman degrading herself for being fat sends the message that health is not the goal—thinness is. A woman with a healthy sex life joking about how she's a slut sends the message that anything short of total abstinence is abject moral failure. Thus, it might seem as if Amy's self-deprecation reinforces the values behind slut-shaming and body-shaming, among other things.

Laughing with Amy at "Amy"

This creates a bit of an incongruity, because as we know from her show, her stand-up, her book, and her movies, Amy doesn't live up to these values, and that doesn't seem to bother her. And yet, her jokes are based on the idea that she should. So, how do we reconcile this incongruity? How can Amy be Amy and enjoy being Amy while also seeming to hate Amy?

One possible solution would be to make a distinction between Amy Schumer and "Amy Schumer"; that is, we could distinguish between Amy Schumer the person and "Amy Schumer" the persona. Amy Schumer is a comedian, writer, and actress, while "Amy Schumer" is her on-stage comic personality.

Amy Schumer makes the jokes. "Amy Schumer" is the butt of the jokes. This theory allows for Amy to be Amy and like being Amy, while condemning "Amy" and everything she stands for. Amy is the hardworking, witty comedian who's forged a successful career for herself in the male-dominated world of comedy, while "Amy" is the morally progressive partier who dares to eat pasta, much to Amy's chagrin.

What does this get us? Really, it explains why self-deprecating humor is safe. When we laugh at a self-deprecator, we aren't laughing at them. By being self-deprecators, they've taken that opportunity away from us. Instead, we laugh with the self-deprecator at their humorous "other." This being, like "Amy Schumer," is purely fictitious. As such, they can't be hurt or degraded or demeaned. Likewise, because of the humorous "other," the self-deprecator can no longer be harmed. They have their humorous "other" to shield them.

The humorous "other" seems like an ideal way to preserve your self-respect while making fun of yourself. Unfortunately, it's a flawed solution. The humorous "other" can't be completely detached from the self-deprecator; otherwise, the whole exercise ceases to make sense. When I'm standing up there mocking myself for my own actions, I really can't separate that self from me, no matter how many logical contortions I perform. If Amy Schumer didn't share at least some characteristics in common with "Amy Schumer," then the self-deprecating jokes wouldn't be *self*-deprecating jokes.

So, in making jokes about her humorous "other," comedian Amy Schumer is still running down comedian Amy Schumer. She still validates the same standards that she doesn't live up to, and she therefore encourages the same sort of shaming. "Amy Schumer" may be worse about living up to those standards, but her very existence tells us that those standards are right, and that anyone who fails to live up to them is a proper object of ridicule—including Amy Schumer.

Last Fuckable Day

The core idea of the superiority theory is the idea of the butt. Every joke has to be about some person or thing. The criticisms of Amy Schumer's humor hinge on the idea that the butt of Amy's self-deprecating jokes is Amy herself. The only way to reconcile self-deprecation with self-respect is to show that a self-deprecating joke can have someone or something other than yourself as the butt. If you thought that there was something a bit off about the superiority theory of humor, you were right. Give yourself a big round of applause, and quit being so hard on yourself all the time!

You can be funny without cutting down yourself or another person in some feeble attempt to make yourself feel good by celebrating all the boring values held dear by the most humorless moralizers. It is not only possible to be funny without being an asshole, but that is in fact the essence of Amy Schumer's form of self-deprecation. Cleverly constructed self-deprecating jokes can be used to make a butt out of *the standards* that the joke seems to espouse. This, I think, is precisely how Amy Schumer's self-deprecating jokes should be understood.

This comes out clearly in some of the sketches on *Inside Amy Schumer*. Two sketches from the third season are of particular relevance here: "Last Fuckable Day" and "12 Angry Men Inside Amy Schumer." "Last Fuckable Day" isn't self-deprecating; it's explicitly a commentary on the standards of feminine beauty. But it nicely sets up the more extended joke of "12 Angry Men Inside Amy Schumer." In "Last Fuckable Day," Amy is invited to join Tina Fey, Julia Louis-Dreyfus, and Patricia Arquette for a party celebrating Julia Louis-Dreyfus's last fuckable day—that is, the last day that Julia Louis-Dreyfus of *Seinfeld*, *The New Adventures of Old Christine*, *Curb Your Enthusiasm,* and *Veep* fame (and one of the most talented comedic actresses of her generation), is deemed to be sexually desirable by Hollywood and the press. The women proceed to explain how someone knows when they've reached their last fuckable day, and why men never have such a day.

"12 Angry Men Inside Amy Schumer" expands on this premise, and gives it a self-deprecating twist by making Amy herself the subject of debate. In the sketch, an all-male jury debates whether Amy is hot enough to be on TV. It plays on some of the same self-deprecating themes we see in her standup, but by delving into them more, the episode manages to turn the joke around. It's no longer a joke about Amy's supposed undesirability, but about the ludicrous standards of beauty women are held to and the ridiculous double standards of attractiveness on TV. The real objects of ridicule are the twelve angry jurors—they are the butts of the joke.

During the course of the jury's deliberations, the entire case boils down to the question of one man's chub and whether it is, indeed, reasonable. The worth and value of a talented writer, actress, and comedian is summed up in the question of whether she's attractive enough to cause a middle-aged man to have an erection. The entirety of the sketch deprecates Amy's appearance—even the positive outcome of the case. The jury finally determines that she is, in fact, hot enough to be on TV, but only on basic cable.

There's even an odd sort of meta-joke that plays on Schumer's self-deprecating material to make a point about double standards. Some of the jurors make a point of the content of Schumer's act, calling her "a filthy whore-mouth" and proclaiming that the fact that she talks openly about her sex life makes her less attractive. When one of the other jurors notes that that kind of talk only makes up a small part of Schumer's stand-up, the critic announces, "Well, then she's worse than a whore. She's a tease! Clowning around up on stage, yapping about her clam without using it." If she's honest about her sex life, she's a whore. If she's joking about it, she's a tease. Short of becoming a nun, there's no way she can win (and even then, she would be a prude).

When we laugh at these sketches, we're not laughing at Amy, or even at "Amy." We're laughing at the values being upheld. They, and not the subject of self-deprecation, are what are being held up for ridicule. To put it in terms of superiority theory, the values of chastity, sobriety, and thinness, and those who try to impose them, are the butt of the joke.

Shocker! . . . Is My Nickname

It's obvious in Schumer's sketches that the butt of the joke is no person, but instead some outdated value. Less obvious is how this interpretation can be applied to the jokes in Schumer's stand-up. The sketch provides a distance between Schumer the joke-teller and Schumer the person. The same distance isn't present, or at least is not immediately obvious, in her stand-up. By putting the jokes in someone else's mouth, these sketches make Schumer sympathetic. In her stand-up, she is both joke-teller and butt of the joke, and we seem to align with the joke-teller and against the butt. That alignment, in turn, means our worry again arises that Schumer's self-deprecating jokes affirm the values they're based on and encourage shaming. Or so it seems.

If we dig a bit deeper, we can see that the same dynamic is at play in Schumer's stand-up and in the sketches from *Inside Amy Schumer*. It's just a bit less obvious in her stand-up. The first temptation here is to revive the distinction between Amy Schumer and "Amy Schumer," but we should avoid this distinction, at least in the form it was made above. In fact, the key to understanding how Schumer's self-deprecating jokes can be self-affirming depends on denying any such distinction. What I have in mind is something like this: when I make a self-deprecating joke about my bad handwriting, I seem to be saying that people should have good handwriting. You could go so far as to say that my self-deprecating joke is an implicit promise that I will work on my handwriting. I'm acknowledging the standard, and the fact that I fall well short of it. The logical next step would be for me to try to meet the standard in the future by improving my handwriting. If I don't, then you could use the joke that I made to justify shaming me.

But we both know that I'm not making any sort of promise. I have no intention of improving my handwriting, and you have no expectation that I would or should do so. Why not? Because I made a joke about it. In this case, there's no possibility of a separation between me as the joke-teller and me as the butt of the joke. The joke-teller's handwriting isn't any better than the butt's.

At the same time, I don't expect you to think that I genuinely feel bad about my awful handwriting. I don't feel bad about it. I barely think about it. (Really, who writes things out by hand anymore, anyway?) Despite appearances, I'm not the butt of my self-deprecating joke. Instead, I'm using self-deprecation to make light of the standard and anyone who might try to shame me for my crappy handwriting. I'm protecting myself, but not by beating my would-be shamer to the punch. I'm protecting myself by letting them know that I don't take the standard itself seriously. Really, when it seems that I'm insulting myself by criticizing my own handwriting, I'm really criticizing the very notion that we should take the standard seriously. I'm not mocking myself. I'm not mocking some other representation of myself. I'm mocking a standard that we use to judge people.

Similarly, Amy Schumer's self-deprecating jokes are a kind of signal that the standards involved in them, and shamers who would uphold them, are ridiculous. So, for example, when Amy tells us, "I love New York, because I can catch a D here kind of whenevs. I was in LA for a while and, um, can't. Can't there" (*Live at the Apollo*), the joke isn't about her appearance, but about the ludicrous standards of beauty and attractiveness maintained in Los Angeles.

To be clear, I'm not claiming that all self-deprecating jokes work like this. Only the good ones do. Bad self-deprecating jokes make the joke-teller the butt of the joke, and call only for a cruel sort of laughter or pity. But good self-deprecating jokes make the standards they call upon the butt of the joke, and encourage the realization that those standards are empty. By joking about our "failings," we show that they're not failings at all.

The Only Time I Get Hit On Is Last Call

The line between good and bad self-deprecation is no doubt a fine one and easy to cross. You could make the case that Amy Schumer's self-deprecating jokes occasionally stagger drunkenly across it. But, in general and for the most part, Amy's self-deprecating jokes are good ones. They appear to make herself the butt of the joke, but in fact poke fun at shamers and their standards.

By making those standards ridiculous, Amy's jokes confront and undermine shaming, and affirm the value of the joke-teller herself. She is in fact "brave"—not for posting a picture of herself in her underwear, but for making fun of those who called her brave for doing it.

3
Schumer's Selfishness

ROBERT ARP

> People have such a low threshold for women being sexual and selfish and human.
>
> —AMY SCHUMER, as quoted in the *Seattle Times* (July 10th 2015)

> We don't need comedy that presents women as selfish, out-of-control, and sex-obsessed.
>
> —KATIE YODER, *Fox News Opinion* (July 16th 2015)

The two defining characteristics of selfishness are being concerned excessively or exclusively with oneself and having no regard for the needs or feelings of others.

We hate it in real life when people are selfish jerks, and we love to see selfish jerks get their just desserts in stories and on film. But comedians will often portray a character as being an over-the-top selfish jerk, and that makes us laugh, because it's just so abnormal, uncomfortable, or perhaps that character reminds us of someone we know—maybe even ourselves!

We all have either been selfish jerks at one point or another, or know someone who's kind of a chronic selfish jerk. Amy Schumer portrays characters who are over-the-top selfish jerks, and we laugh our asses off. I look at Schumer's performances as not only having entertainment value, but also having educational value as examples of how *not* to live your life.

But a *lot* of Schumer's characters—and her mockeries of herself in comedy sketches—are selfish jerks, which causes us to think of a kind of philo-psycho-sociological question: Is it possible to ever act on a motivation that's *not* selfish? In the first episode of Season Two of *Inside Amy Schumer* ("You Would Bang Her?"), even God himself (played by Paul Giamatti) is amazed at how selfish Schumer is and how she won't even "make a small sacrifice" like calling her mother more often.

If we take a cold, hard, *objective* look at ourselves, isn't it true that we'll only do something if we benefit from it? More precisely, *I'll* only do something if *and only* if *me, myself, and I* benefit from it—if there's no benefit in it for me, then I'm not doing it.

Egoists, Every Last One of Them

Most of us know that the Latin word *ego* means "self" or "I", because the famous psychoanalyst Sigmund Freud (1856–1939) started using the term to describe the human psyche (along with the *id* and the *superego*) by the turn of the twentieth century. Now it's commonplace to equate selfish jerks with *ego*ists (or *ego*tists), *ego*maniacs, or *ego*tistical jerks. There's actually a view called *psychological egoism*, which holds that self-interest is the sole motivator of human action. In other words, according to this view, people ultimately only act in order to benefit themselves; *nothing else* is even capable of driving human action.

On the face of it, this seems correct. We're all naturally concerned with our own welfare, security, and happiness. In *The Theory of Moral Sentiments* (1759) at III.I.46, Adam Smith talks about how Europeans would react to the news of people being killed in a Chinese earthquake. (Adam Smith is a famous moral and political philosopher, the pioneer of the modern science of economics, and also the guy who coined the phrase "the invisible hand" to capture the unintended social benefits of allowing individuals to engage in self-interested actions as much as they want to.) Of course, European folks would feel badly, but let's face it:

> The most frivolous disaster which could befall himself would occasion a more real disturbance. If he was to lose his little finger to-morrow, he would not sleep to-night; but, provided he never saw them (the Chinese), he will snore with the most profound security over the ruin of a hundred millions of his brethren, and the destruction of that immense multitude seems plainly an object less interesting to him, than this paltry misfortune of his own.

The point is that if something doesn't affect us in some way directly, we don't really care much about it.

There are countless examples of actual events—many now caught on tape and shown on reality TV shows—where a person is getting mugged, or knifed to death, or is run over by a car, and people witnessing the event (or the aftermath) do nothing but watch as the horrible events unfold. When asked afterward why they did not help the victim, the typical response of the onlooker is, "Hey, I'm not gonna risk my life," or "It's not my problem."

The final episode of the TV show *Seinfeld* emphasizes this seeming self-centeredness, when Seinfeld and his cohorts witness someone getting mugged and, instead of helping out in any way by screaming at the mugger or calling for help (easy things to do), they watch the mugging and crack jokes!

In July of 2017, five teenagers in Cocoa Beach, Florida watched as a man drowned in a pond near his family's home, and one of the teens decided to videotape the experience. No one lifted a finger to help the drowning man, and they didn't call the police. They did, however, post the two-minute-long video to YouTube, where they can be heard laughing, snickering, and saying, "You gonna die," and, "We ain't helpin' yo ass," as well as chortling, "He's dead," during the victim's final moments.

Amy Schumer makes a joke of this kind of selfishness, like in the sketch "9/11", in which she's more concerned about her sandwich and Verizon's cell signal than she is about the story her friend is telling her about where he was on 9/11 (a tragedy with which I'm sure we're all familiar).

Self-Aware of Selfishness

But wait a minute. You mean there's no other reason why someone will act? Not for God? Country? Love? According to the psychological egoist, if it appears that someone is acting *altru*istically or for any other non-selfish reason, that's only because doing so *ultimately* is of benefit to the self. In fact, most of the time, we're unaware of the fact that this is what's really going on.

In several of the editions of his textbook, *The Elements of Moral Philosophy*, the late great James Rachels recounts a legend about Abraham Lincoln, who supposedly was once riding in a carriage with a friend and arguing that we are all ultimately self-interested, when he stopped to save a group of piglets from drowning while their mother was squealing and looking on. Lincoln's friend praised him for acting purely altruistically, but Lincoln responded by saying something like, "What I did was actually the epitome of selfishness, because I would have been wracked with guilt all day had I gone on and left that suffering old sow worrying over those baby pigs. I did it to get my own peace of mind, don't you see?" The psychological egoist would praise Lincoln for being so self-aware.

Several of Schumer's skits and movie roles have a lot of fun with this idea—that the people with whom Schumer (or her character) interacts *think* that she's doing something kind or generous on their behalf, when we the viewers know that Schumer's *really* just using the person for her own personal gain or pleasure. In the sketch, "Cancer Excuse," Amy's character finds out that one of her writers (Tig Notaro) has cancer, and she proceeds to use *someone else's cancer* as an excuse to make selfish demands. In the movie *Snatched*, Schumer's character Emily Middleton convinces her mother to come on a trip to Ecuador with her using a line, "C'mon mom! This will be good for you." But in actuality, Emily doesn't want to go alone or lose the deposit on the trip.

Mother Teresa . . . That Selfish Beyatch!

Speaking of moms, you would think that their sacrifice and love for their children—even to the point of dying for them, in some cases—would indicate that they're not selfish. But that's not so, according to the psychological egoist. Even moms are selfish. There's no way they could live with themselves if they *didn't* take care of, sacrifice for, or even die for their children. They couldn't live with the guilt, and they certainly couldn't live with the stigma of other mothers thinking or saying, "Some mother she is! She let her daughter die!"

And that other famous mother, Mother Teresa, who gave up a comfy life, became a nun, established leprosy-outreach clinics throughout Calcutta, did all kinds of other unbelievably kind-hearted things for poor, sick, and dying people, and was canonized as a saint in the Catholic Church in 2016? She's one of the most selfish persons who ever lived! Why? Because she did everything she did so she could get into Heaven! What's a mere seventy years of pain in this world when you can live forever in bliss in the next? "Don't be fooled by the altruistic veneer," notes the psychological egoist, "We all are only doing things that give us some kind of benefit, pleasure, good, or satisfaction."

Since Plato, thinkers have been struggling with whether humans are all basically selfish jerks or not, along the lines of what the psychological egoist believes. It's hard to swallow this idea that everybody *only* will act if there's some kind of benefit for the self. The psychological egoist might say that the first responders who ran into the Twin Towers on 9/11/2001 only to be literally pulverized in the rubble as the towers came crashing down, or the man who was hit and killed by a train in Modesto, California, on Tuesday, March 29th 2016 while saving a dog that ran onto the train tracks, or the Texas mom who drowned saving her daughter from being carried away by a rushing current during Hurricane Harvey in the summer of 2017, were all "really just performing selfish actions." In each of these cases, some kind of *personal* pleasure or pain was supposedly motivating these folks to act.

In other words, for the psychological egoist, there's no way *whatsoever* that a person *could* be anything other than self-concerned, whether it's with gaining personal pleasure or avoiding personal pain. You could respond back to the psychological egoist with more examples of people who seem to act selflessly—the guy who was killed by the rapist while coming to the aid of a girl being raped, the woman who fell through the ice and died trying to save the stranger who had already fallen through the ice and was screaming for help, the captain who gave up his rations so that a member of his crew could eat while several of them were lost on a lifeboat at sea for a month—and the egoist will always respond with: "It *looks* as if someone is being selfless, but deep down it's basic self-preservation and/or self-interest that motivates anyone."

But these actions don't strike us in the same way as do the actions of the murderer, rapist, kidnapper, extortionist, or serial robber who's doing time in a maximum-security prison. And what about Charles Ponzi (1882–1949), of Ponzi scheme fame? (Google *Ponzi scheme*—this guy was a real c@cksucker). Consider Bernie Madoff. He was the chairman of the NASDAQ stock market for a while, as well as the admitted operator of a Ponzi scheme that is considered to be the largest financial fraud in US history, with estimated actual losses to investors of $18 billion! On June 29th 2009 Madoff was sentenced to 150 years in prison, the maximum allowed for such a selfishly jerkish crime. Some people who lost money as a result of Madoff's Ponzi scheme committed suicide, others died of heart attacks, most had to alter their lavish lifestyles, all are still fighting legal battles today to recover at least some of their investments, one died of a stroke, and at least one elderly person has lost so much that she has had to eat cat food in order to survive. Now Madoff seems like a total douche and the epitome of a selfish jerk. But it's hard to imagine that the Long Island mom who pushed her child out of the way of a speeding car on Mother's Day in 2017 after leaving a bakery in Lindenhurst, New York—only to save her child and get run over dead herself in the process—was acting purely out of a selfish reason! There seems to be a big difference here between that mother and when Amy Schumer decides to fuck a prom loser, because her selfish attempt to appear selfless by advertising for PETA has backfired ("Publicity Stunt").

Possibly Back Assward?

Also, it seems that the psychological egoist has things back assward. Personal pleasures or pains are not always motivators for what we do—in fact, they're mostly by-products, or consequences, of what we do. (I'm not talking about going out and seeking pleasure specifically, as in a one-night stand situation.) Jane doesn't stop to help the drowning children *in order to get* the satisfaction that follows from saving a life, Frank doesn't assist the blind person across the Manhattan street *in order to get* the satisfaction that follows from doing a good deed, and Emily Middleton (Amy's character in *Snatched*) didn't assist the residents of the Colombian village *in order to get* the satisfaction that follows from her having helped them get water from the well. Instead, Jane, Frank, and Emily are motivated by folks in need, and not some satisfaction they knew they were going to be gaining from having performed the actions.

That said, I'm no Sigmund Freud. The decision-making process is a highly complex, subtle, and self-deceptive process. Indeed, psychologists and neuroscientists tell us that motivation is often so influenced by brain chemistry that we don't ourselves know why we do the things we do; it's not always completely transparent to us what our motives are. And lots of times our actions don't follow from deliberation, but rather from sheer habit, and much mental activity is unconscious, subconscious, non-conscious, or some-other-kind-of conscious that's unaware of what's going on. So, it may be that the whole question of what truly motivates human action is pointless to ask, because it's hard (perhaps impossible, given that we're talking about minds) to get at what *exactly* really motivates people to act in certain situations.

Types of Selfishness

I've pointed out that the two defining characteristics of selfishness are being concerned excessively or exclusively with oneself and having no regard for the needs or feelings of others.

It seems that Mother Teresa, the 9/11 first responders, the dog lover, the mom who died in Hurricane Harvey, and the mom who died on Mother's Day don't really fit this description, but people like murderers, rapists, serial robbers, Ponzi, Madoff, and those Cocoa Beach teens who laughed and snickered while they taped a man drowning and placed the video on YouTube *do* fit this description.

We can make some distinctions here. The following four statements are all attempts to capture the idea of psychological egoism. Yet these statements are not the same; they're *different*.

1. ***I always and only act due to automatic self-preservation.***
2. ***I always and only act due to an un- or non-conscious, learned motivation where I get something out of it.***
3. ***I always and only act due to a conscious motivation where I get something out of it, realizing others may get something out of it too.***
4. ***I always and only act due to a conscious motivation where I get something out of it, and I give a rat's ass if anyone else gets anything out of it or not—in fact, it's probably better that they don't.***

If the psychological egoist has #1 in mind, then it's trivially true, since self-preservation is basic for any animal, and humans are no different. Evolutionary biologists have documented a gazillion cases of kin selection too, where the reproductive success of an organism's relatives are favored, even at a cost to the organism's own survival and reproduction. A squirrel or ape might make a noise to warn others of a predator, even though it draws the attention of the predator to it and is eaten; but the rest of the squirrels or apes get to survive. Similarly, a human mother probably instinctually saves her baby to preserve her own species.

If the psychological egoist has #2 in mind, then this is more interesting, for sure. As the description suggests, I *learn* to be self-concerned, self-absorbed, selfie-loving, and self-insulated—after all, it's a dog-eat-dog world out there. But even this so-called "learned" behavior could be the result of evolutionary processes, since it's well known that memes—elements of a culture or system of behavior that are passed from one individual to another by non-genetic means, especially imitation—as well as genes drive animals, especially the great apes.

But humans have a unique place in the biological kingdom, because we have (apparently) conscious minds and (apparent) free will. If we accept this as a given, then it's #3 and #4 that are really up for debate. Many would argue that #3 is true, and there are even entire schools of thought devoted to this way of thinking, such as *rational choice theory* and other kinds of decisions in what is known as *game theory*. The current US President, Donald Trump, has made an "art" out of "the deal" where both parties in an association, partnership, or project gain something in the endeavor. It's probably the case that there's an admixture of egoism in the #3 sense in all of what we consciously do. So, if the psychological egoist has #3 in mind, there's some truth here.

Now #4 is what we have in mind when we think of the typical selfish jerk, a person who's aware of the fact that she or he doesn't care about anybody else's desires, dreams, feelings, and the like. At the end of "9/11," Amy's friend asks her where she was on 9/11, and she doesn't remember. In all fairness, it may be that most selfish jerks aren't really that aware of their selfish jerkiness. Schumer's over-the-top comedy in this regard is so funny *precisely because* she's clueless about her selfish jerkiness. Consider the opening scenes of *Snatched*, where we think Emily is shopping for clothes for her trip to Ecuador, and then we find out she's actually the salesperson in the store! It's funny as sh!t when she's called out by her boss for her actions, but she doesn't "get it" that she's supposed to be serving the customers' needs and not the other way around. Same with the *Inside Amy Schumer* sketch, "Herpes Scare" (that has Paul Giamatti as God). God's so astonished at how cluelessly selfish Schumer is that he remarks, "I gotta quit making white girls."

From Psychological to Ethical

Psychological egoism is a *descriptive* view that isn't making any sort of value judgment about what has worth, what's right or wrong, good or bad, nor is it prescribing anything about what we should or ought to do. Rather, it simply describes human psychology and what motivates human action.

However, *should* everything we do or not do always and at all times be done with an eye toward our own personal benefit or pay-off? If you answer *yes* to this question, then you're likely someone who buys into *ethical egoism*. Ethical egoism is a *prescriptive* view with an argument that goes something like this:

> **Premise #1:** Look around you: it's a dog-eat-dog, rat race, Darwinian, cruel-ass kind of world. Each and every person is always out for his/her own good, and, further, you will get screwed over by people if you don't look out for your own good.
>
> **Premise #2:** If it's true that every person is always out for his/her own good, then each one of us *should* be out for our own personal good.
>
> **Conclusion:** Therefore, each one of us *should* always be out for our own personal good. In other words, we should all be ethical egoists.

However, the argument for ethical egoism has been critiqued and rejected for a number of reasons. First off, the part of

Premise #1 that goes "Each and every person is always out for his/her own good" is debatable, as we've talked about already. Is it really true that each and every person is *always* out for his/her own good? *Always*? And it's also debatable whether "it's a dog-eat-dog, rat race, Darwinian, cruel-ass kind of world," and "you will get screwed over by people if you don't look out for your own good" are true—at least, it's debatable whether they hold *in every single human interaction*, such that they're to be treated like scientific laws of nature on a par with what goes up must come down!

More Problems . . .

There are many problems with Premise #2 of the ethical egoism argument, but we'll just mention a practical one here, followed by a corresponding logical problem (which is the basis for another kind of practical problem). First, just because something *is* the case, does not mean that it *should be* or *ought to be* the case, which I am sure we have all heard on more than one occasion. For example:

- **Just because it *is* the case that the class does not want to take the final exam does not mean that they *shouldn't* take the final exam. The final is likely integral to the class and the grading system utilized, for example.**
- **Just because it *is* the case that you want a fifth piece of cake does not mean that you *should* have the fifth piece of cake, for obvious BMI and other health reasons.**
- **Just because it *is* the case that someone "turns you on" does not mean that you *should* sleep with them, especially if you're married (to someone else)!**

So too, even if it were the case that everybody were a self-centered devil in a society, this does not mean that they *should* act devilish toward one another. In fact, to a certain extent, there are "little devils" running around already: they're called children. Kids are naturally self-centered, but that doesn't mean that they should be. When Sally kicks Johnny in the package for no good reason at school, Ms. Smith the teacher doesn't say, "Kick him again, Sally, then punch him in the kidney while he's rolling on the ground in pain, so he wets himself!" Amy's nephew Allistair, in *Trainwreck*, is hilarious just because he's *not* that kind of typical selfish jerk that all kids usually are.

There's also a corresponding *logical* problem related to the *practical* one just mentioned. If ethical egoism were enacted in a society, there would be no way to adjudicate any kind of perceived offense. Sally could say, "For *me*, according to *my* own moral perspective, it's moral for *me* to lie to you, Johnny," while at the same time Johnny could say, "For *me*, according *my* own moral perspective, it's not moral for you to lie to me, Sally." The same action, lying, would be both right and wrong at the same time—and this would be the case for any value judgments we make. The result would be total chaos in any society, because there would no objective, third-party way to decide *logically* who's right and who's wrong. So, ethical egoism would not only actually lead to total chaos, but it's wholly inconsistent logically as a principled guide for moral actions . . . which would lead to total chaos anyway!

That's Entertainment

The argument for ethical egoism is a bad one and should be rejected. We should not strive to be ethical egoists, if that means being concerned excessively or exclusively with oneself and having no regard for the needs or feelings of others. And although the psychological egoist is right about the fact that there are a lot of selfish jerks in this world, we should strive to confront and stop any real-life selfish jerk we encounter; for example, a bully.

My fourteen-year-old daughter is a second-degree black belt in Tae Kwon Do, and I tell her to go ahead and stick up for her friends and herself in the face of some selfish jerk, even if it means planting the right side of her right foot on the left side of the selfish jerk's face at around eighty-five m.p.h. Does that bring me pleasure, knowing that she can do that? H3ll yes! Am I motivated by my own selfish desires to see her succeed as a reflection of my own success, such that I live vicariously through her, and because I was bullied on the playground as a kid I want to make sure she's never bullied or comes to the aid of someone who's bullied by kicking their ass? Easy, Sigmund . . .

Because there's always a little bit of self-interest in anything we do (otherwise, we wouldn't do it), maybe what we should do is aim at some kind of rational, enlightened self-interest, as opposed to crass selfishness. Those rational choice theory folks and invisible hand economists are on to something here. This might be not only personally liberating but also socially beneficial.

Of course, we can still desire that crass selfishness be part of our entertainment, and on that score, Schumer is *definitely* entertaining.

4
To Be or Not to Be Perfect?

KAREN FLIESWASSER

Everybody seems to have an opinion on what it means to be perfect. From the Hollywood movies we watch to the values we're taught in school, it seems that the world around us is desperately trying to guide us toward perfecting our sorry human selves. And the funny (or sad) part is that we actually seem to fall for their so-called "guidance," adjusting ourselves to the expectations we're held against so that we can finally appear to be a little more perfect.

Getting an Ivy League degree, maintaining flawless skin, and always greeting people politely are all things that I could strive to do, in order to become what advocates of perfection call "a better version of myself"—perhaps even a happier version!

But is chasing perfection truly worth it? (And worth *what?*) After all, we're imperfect from the second we're born. From the inherited flaws of our parents to the broken environment we might grow up in, we're almost naturally bound to be imperfect. And yet, sometimes it may seem like society is built upon this idea that we'll all be better off if only we try to be better than the messes that we are.

I beg to differ. I beg to ponder the question of whether we actually *don't* become better off by striving for perfection.

The seemingly endless road to full perfection is so filled with misery, failure, and just the acceptance of an often quite brutal reality, that hopelessly aspiring to become perfect in some way despite all that seems almost a bit crazy. Trying the same thing multiple times won't help you to achieve a different result. I'm thinking that maybe this logic applies to striving for perfection as well.

If I'll be using the same, recommended ways to try to achieve a higher level of perfection, then I'm most likely just going to run in circles and feel really bad about it. However, if I remove myself from the chains of suggested ways to become a better and happier person, then maybe I'll be able to explore different routes to self-fulfillment, and to what I believe will be my own standards of perfection. (And then, once I do discover the road to what I conceive of as perfection, I can be a perfectionist about that all I want.)

My Own Kind of Perfect

Now, before I continue talking about the distinction I just made, I of course want to bring up Amy Schumer. Not just because this is a book about Amy Schumer, but because her comedy really resonates with what I'm about to say here.

Whether you consider her to be a feminist, a rebel or just an obnoxious jokester, after watching some of her work, you'd probably agree with the statement that Amy Schumer really doesn't care too much for external standards (like having to be thin, modest, and perhaps even submissive). She mocks her past self for falling for them, embraces her present self for getting over them, and she urges her audience to do the same!

She's always, one hundred percent, for just embracing yourself and accepting that, if you learn from your mistakes, then it is *absolutely okay* to make them. She doesn't even apologize for the silly things she says and does, living with the simple fact that, hey, stupidity is just part of humanity, and no matter how much you practice, you're going to perform imperfectly at times in life.

There's a peaceful quality to the message behind Amy Schumer's humor, because it's telling you to just stop caring so much about what others think of you, and to start caring more about what *you* think of you. And with this ode to humble self-love, I want to take us back to where I left off—a distinction that I've drawn between what I called "suggested" paths to perfection and developing my own standards of perfection.

Let me just remind you right away of how pervasive these "suggested" paths are, and that they're not soft-spoken at all. In fact, receiving countless random images from various screens on various devices about how my hair or body should look is quite an aggressive kind of messaging, especially when I receive these messages on a daily basis (together with the other millions of women). And when I go to career counselors, and they all tell me that getting a degree in X is the best thing on earth right now, it's pretty pressuring to think that if I'd want to study something else, I'm going to have to hear from some wise noses why I'll fail at life until the end of my degree.

All of these ideas, the ubiquitous ones about what it takes to be perfect, can get pretty scary, especially when you don't have the energy to fight them all off. They start circling in your head and getting the best of you, sort of pushing your own self-esteem down before you even get a chance to build it up. Imagine that all of these words, coming from everyone, about how to be better, and about why you're currently not good enough, are put on pause for a while. What would that feel like? You'd wake up in the morning, and it would start with not judging yourself so much while looking in the mirror. You'd assemble an outfit that you personally like, without too much regard for what your mother or boss might say, and you'd skip out the door with a piece of food that nobody screamed at you for eating (or not eating). And you've really put thought and care into the way you braided your hair, wrapped your scarf, and picked the right fruit for you to eat, because you've slowly gotten to know yourself over the years while the noise was gone. To you, perfection has gotten a new meaning. Maybe instead of a Starbucks morning coffee, you've just learned that your body likes Indian tea more around that time of day. And you're absolutely cool with that, because nobody forcefully asks you to revise your opinion about yourself at every opportunity.

When I read Amy Schumer's *The Girl with The Lower Back Tattoo*, I almost felt like she's living that kind of life today, where she's gradually become more at peace with herself and found her place in the world. That seems like a comforting mental space to be in—one she's claimed to fight hard for. I suppose this is what makes Amy Schumer relatable, because in the end, we're all that flawed human being who's just kind of tired of always trying to be perfect according to other people's random wishes. We're a lot more empowered when we get to have our own say on things, especially when that "thing" is our own minds and bodies. There's something humbling about this journey towards self-acceptance, and once you learn to accept and embrace yourself, you're also more open to do the same for others.

One of the comments that sticks with me the most, from *The Girl with The Lower Back Tattoo*, is when Amy recalls how tough it was for her to realize that her parents are just fragile human beings. To look at the people who made you, and to think, "Well, you guys aren't so great after all," is an indirect way of reflecting on ourselves as well, admitting that we're not always amazing, and maybe that we don't always have to be superman or superwoman to still be experienced as good parents or good human beings.

There's a cliché, "Beauty is in the eye of the beholder", and I wonder if that saying has got something to do with this act of coming to terms with ourselves (and reducing the noises around us that tell us to just be more impossibly perfect already). In the end, if you think of yourself as beautiful, and the people around you who value you do so as well, then maybe that's what matters most. Who cares what that Photoshopped lady on the billboard thinks of me? That's the spirit, I say, and I think that Amy Schumer's comedy conveys exactly this message: Embrace yourself, because in the end, what others are asking of you when they're demanding pure perfection is nearly impossible, as you're just human (and that's okay).

Still Struggling with Imperfection

I guess that message really stands out in the series *Inside Amy Schumer*, where she seems to take a point of departure that involves some ridiculous idea of perfection common to contemporary American society. There's this one sketch ("Judging Strippers") where a bunch of middle-class ladies look outside their exercise class window to see a couple of female dancers. They're all shocked, saying how sorry they feel for the female dancers, and how awful it must be to objectify their bodies for the sake of pleasure. A few moments later, their teacher calls them to the dancefloor, where they're all jumping on what look like stripper poles. For a moment, you feel like you're not sure anymore what to think of those ladies. They were just feeling sad for female dancers, whom they believed were forced into their profession, only to deliberately jump on stripper poles for the sake of exercise—to look more beautiful and attractive. And yet, these are the same ladies who thought it was awful to objectify the human body for pleasure.

I don't think Amy Schumer is making any comment here on whether it is or isn't cool to be a stripper. I do think that she's implying that the ladies in the episode are acting like hypocrites, because they condone striving for beauty and attraction when it comes to their own bodies, yet they don't condone it when others strive to see it on other women's bodies. In other words, as long as they subject themselves to ridiculous standards, rather than being subjected to them by others, then it's fine by them. I suppose the possibility to choose, in this case, is what gives them a sense of power, even if the choice itself is questionable. In the end, all of the female dancers, their audience, and the ladies in the class are involved in the same act of working the body for beauty, attraction, and pleasure. And if that act seems absurd after watching Amy Schumer's episode, then maybe we've come to some crossroads here, with the following options:

- **Do I completely stop trying to build my body for beauty, attraction, and pleasure? *(Yes, this means I can finally binge eat in front of the TV and never work out again.)***

- **Do I continue to build my body, but try to stop others from enjoying it? *(But this could lead to going to the gym when it's dark and basically living in a dungeon.)***
- **Do I continue to build my body *and* enable others to enjoy it? *(This brings us back to working out on stripper poles and calling it an exercise class.)***

Personally, I would just do away with the stripper poles in an exercise class. I don't particularly favor the idea of certain female dancers, either. But that's just me, and others are entitled to have their own opinions on this subject.

Specifically, the subject of working our bodies, but also working our minds, has garnered lots of attention and elicited a multitude of opinions over the years—pardon me, throughout the centuries. I've only touched upon tiny bits of American culture so far, but discussions about societal versus personal standards of perfection stretch way beyond the United States.

Let's go back to the three options I presented above. The first option demands that I stop trying to work my body for beauty, attraction, and pleasure. This, to me, brings up an image of somebody studious and disciplined, perhaps even religious, who places the life of the soul above that of the body. Instead of working the body, this person really wants to develop their mind. This person's lifestyle already implies some kind of assumption about perfection: that human perfection is reached when the body is left as is and the mind is developed to its maximum potential.

This theme is found in the written thoughts of philosophers like Plato and Descartes, who believe that most of what's essential to us is the human mind, rather than the body. It's our memories, intelligence, and conversations with ourselves that make us who we are—humans always striving to know more. Perfection, then, is the ability to have absolute knowledge about ourselves, other people, and the world—something that seems destined only for the greatest, in the likes of Greek gods, perhaps, or a mad scientist in the midst of a scientific revolution.

Wouldn't Amy Schumer be a better person if she focused on comedy without having to worry about journaling about that smoothie she had for breakfast? Isn't it a little absurd that she has to lose weight in order to star in a movie that *she wrote*, based on *her own* experiences? The idea that we're at our best when our *mind*s are well-trained, with books flowing out of our expanding bookshelves at home and degrees earned at the best institutions, is just one take on what it means to be perfect as human beings. It places the quality of the mind at the top of the priority pyramid, and almost takes human intelligence for granted, thinking that if human intelligence is well-developed, happiness and prosperity follow along, and all is well.

But then again, we've seen examples in the Western world of socially deprived high school students, university graduates who are drowning in debt, and unemployed PhD graduates. In a world where social and economic concerns also reign, is it really wise to unconditionally prioritize human intelligence as being the gateway to our own perfection? Take Amy Schumer herself. She could've rehearsed a million times what it's like to be a well-performing comedienne, after graduating from theater school, proving herself to be studious. But for her to make a mark in the arts, she needed more than book smarts—and she's made it with drive, perseverance, and a hint of feminist obstinacy.

She portrays a similar can-do, borderline rebellious attitude in her movies, depicting often semi-ditzy characters like Amy (a movie character literally bearing the comedienne's own name) in *Trainwreck* who, unlike what her father taught her about the havocs of marriage, ends up following her own voice by pursuing a monogamous relationship. So maybe it takes more than conventional intelligence to succeed, and you need to be working more than just your brain muscles to have a say in this world.

Perhaps the second option is more reasonable and realistic, then, which says to continue working your body and stop others from enjoying it. This sounds a lot like what the monotheistic religions talk about when they issue modesty (especially in the case of female modesty). I completely condone modesty, whether it be intellectual or physical, but how far should modesty go before it's too far? When is modesty ever overrated? In *Amy Schumer: Mostly Sex Stuff*, Amy Schumer tests the boundaries of her audience by taking them through recollections of things that are better left unsaid. Yet she says them, loudly so, speaking of her experiences as funny anecdotes that are, nonetheless, absolutely factual. She doesn't wrap reality in cotton candy, even when it's ugly, confronting us with the ups and downs of her personal encounters. Questions involving modesty, and in particular modesty among women and their sexuality, ring a bell about debates regarding the female veil in Islam, which has entered the Western world and placed it on its uncovered head.

I'm personally fine with skipping the stripper pole shenanigans turned exercise class, and I don't necessarily like how tiny they make bikinis these days, but I also don't want to cover my entire face and body with layers of loose fabric just to be extra sure about others not watching me. In the end, I am who I am, and I do expect a certain level of respect in return for that—one that doesn't require me to hide away in fear of others' every judgment. Plus, in time, societies have proven capable of changing their ways and their views about male and female modesty. Christian women in the West used to be more covered up in the past; some Jewish women around the world still are, to an extent; and there are cultures that practice being topless on a daily basis. All in all, it seems like living a very revealed or an otherwise very private life is largely a matter of historical context, dominant culture, and personal choice. I understand that modesty is something that I can reflect in my clothes, my attitude around others, and the way I carry myself in life, and there's no absolute standard for that.

The third option I presented was to continue working my body and enable others to enjoy it. That can easily sound a little wrong, so allow me to clarify. Working my body can mean keeping fit, eating healthy, and engaging in activities that nurture both body and soul, like doing yoga or taking a hike. Enabling others to enjoy the fruits of my actions doesn't equate to allowing others to abuse me in some way or another. It means that if I labored with my body to build a house, maybe someday someone can live in it and make a home for themselves. Or if my name is Amy Schumer and I dress up in a tight leather suit during one of my shows (*The Leather Special*), I can make people laugh and realize that I don't need to be stick figure skinny to rock a leather suit in public. These are some of the many positive ways that I can imagine, for which the third option works. I just don't really know how to relate it back to perfection, as it seems a bit tricky. What's really the perfect way of being productive and enabling others to be influenced by it positively?

According to Aristotle, the perfect way of developing ourselves for the greater good is by achieving our *telos*—the individual purpose that's within all of us. But who determines our purpose? Does nature place it upon us, or do we come up with it ourselves? Does society dictate my purpose to me, or can I have a small, equal or perhaps larger say in it myself? It seems that even if we do assume to have a purpose, it's kind of hard to figure out who or what decides it, and it's even harder to find out exactly what our individual purposes are. And even if we do discover a purpose for ourselves that isn't entirely arbitrary, who says it is possible to achieve it? And should I not be able to reach my purpose, then is my life considered less worthy all of a sudden?

Perfectly Human, After All

So I've tried devoting my life to expanding my mind, becoming a modest person, and finding my individual purpose. I've also tried a million other causes to live for, all in the ultimate pursuit of perfecting myself, but none of these pathways has felt gratifying to me in the long run. Something was always missing, and I will continue to lack things as I carry on. This eternal burden seems too much to handle, much like the grievances with one's own faith depicted in Shakespeare's tragedy-filled *Hamlet* (referenced in this chapter's title).

Just as Hamlet asked himself whether this meager life was worth it at all, so do I ponder the question whether mine has any perfect meaning, if I am to be flawed and upset with one thing or another forever. As the simple saying goes, shit happens, and if we accept Murphy's Law, then the worst that can happen will most likely happen indeed. But perhaps there's light at the end of the tunnel if we expand our viewpoint.

Philosophers have thought about the value of perfection for a very long time and in almost all corners of the world. We've so far mainly discussed Western ideas, but far away in the East, one idea is waiting for us to discover it. It's the Japanese philosophy of *Wabi-sabi*, where peace of mind and acceptance of the imperfect come together in an artful way of life. Just as Amy Schumer has learned to be *Zen* with herself, so does the philosophy of *Wabi-sabi* (which sounds much like a type of delicious food, yet is not as easy to stomach) call for practicing patience with oneself and finding closure in the world around us.

One of the greatest takeaways from the *Wabi-sabi* philosophy is what the Japanese call the aesthetics of *Kintsugi*. If you've always thought that being vulnerable, flawed, and broken or not the very best is something to be ashamed of, think again! *Kintsugi* artists will glue your broken pieces back together and relish in the newfound beauty of that which is you, and all but uniquely you.

When I think of Amy Schumer and her comedic style, I can't help but think of *Kintsugi*. I imagine that she's taken a good look in the mirror, observing the pieces that are her, and that she's put these pieces together where they belong. She's not embarrassed by the experiences that have shaped these pieces into what they are, and she's not afraid to lay it all on the table and explore her own puzzling existence.

We're all different puzzles, with pieces that latch onto each other, each telling their own story, and revealing something new about ourselves.

II

Schumer the Philosopher

5
The Funny Thing about Being Yourself

GREGOR BALKE

Among all of the things Amy Schumer does, the least expected is something unfunny. Sure, not everything a comedian says has to be funny. That's all right; they're humans, too. But if you look close enough, you'll often recognize that the funniest bits are deeply connected to some serious issues. In *The Girl with the Lower Back Tattoo*, Amy brings to mind her experiences while working as a waitress:

> All those mean chefs who belittled the waiters, and the sociopathic restaurant managers who led with fear and intimidation, wielding their minuscule amount of power to scare the shit out of any employee who needed a day off for even the most legit of reasons . . . All those assholes really showed me several specific versions of who I didn't want to become if I was ever in charge. (p. 126)

In those reflections lies no joke. There's nothing funny in what she's saying. But it nevertheless sums up the attitude of Amy Schumer's approach to comedy and life. It shows how Amy deals with bad experiences and transforms them into the ability to be a better person—and to be a funny person as well.

Amy has had to find her own voice, all the while dealing with the frightening fact of being a public figure. But of course, you are not simply there, all of a sudden, on a stage, a screen, or a book cover. To get there means that you had to become that person. And that touches on the philosophical issue of identity and the sometimes uneasy ways a person discovers or enacts their own identity.

The Story of Telling the Story of Yourself

Becoming who you are involves the ability to create a narrative about yourself. Creating your own narrative is something everyone does, whether it's at work, at home, or in a relationship; we tell stories about our lives in order to create a coherent picture of ourselves. This doesn't say anything about the honesty or dishonesty of these stories. It merely describes how we tend to present ourselves in front of others.

Just ask Amy how Bradley Cooper became her boyfriend. It's not an easy thing, to be successful at making a self-created narrative. It does not suffice just to tell personal stories. There's much more to it. Amy Schumer is a master at creating a genuine and authentic comedy persona. At first, this sounds inconsistent, because we assume that authenticity is connected with truthfulness, frankness, and realness. You know, all of the qualities that Amy embodies on stage. But she is still putting on a show. Amy is a performer who's giving a performance, and that involves disguising, or at least not being up front about everything she is feeling or going through on a particular day. When she's up on stage Amy is adopting a *persona*. And that's fine—that's the whole idea behind performance. It's the *persona* that audiences find hilarious.

Persona is derived from the Latin word for "mask." When we're interacting with people, we put on our (hopefully) socially-acceptable masks and live our lives. So it's not a question about who Amy Schumer really is, which is none of our business anyway. It's about how Amy shares her stories with us and tells a story about herself in order to reach that narrative self-creation. It's all about the comedic persona she displays on stage, on television, in the movies, throughout her book, and even on her Instagram. Amy evolves her narrative self in a splendid and remarkable way. And that's why she teaches us something about identity and the art of self-creation, without telling us every private aspect of her life (even though she does that every now and then).

One time, Amy Schumer shared a photo taken by Annie Leibovitz on social media. Amy describes it in her *Leather Special* (2017) on Netflix:

> I'm holding a coffee, I'm topless in just underwear, and it goes viral. Like it was everywhere, every news show, every website. And that's when I learned the word you don't want people to use when a nude photo of you goes viral: brave.

This is Amy at her best. She's smart, funny (of course), and most importantly, vulnerable. In posting the photo and relating the anecdote, Amy is radically honest with herself, in front of us. This sort of radical honesty is no easy (or quick) achievement. It's a statement of one's identity that some people never get the courage to make. It was probably no easy feat for Amy to get to the place in her life where she had enough self-assurance—where she was comfortable enough with her own identity—to express herself to the world. We are not just dealing in metaphors when we say that creating one's identity is quite a journey.

In addition to adopting the persona of a widely-talented comedian, Amy is a person who shares precious insights into her own journey. She transforms these insights into something we can all enjoy: comedy, laughter, and a good bunch of dirty jokes. She tells us her story.

The Problem of Being There . . . Forever

Amy's comedy reveals something the German philosopher Friedrich Nietzsche (1844–1900) brought to the fore within the history of philosophy. Nietzsche never did pursue his philosophy as a closed system of principles. Instead, he chose an elliptical way of approaching his subject matter, like a bird that has spotted something on the ground.

Nietzsche loved to speak in metaphors and linguistic images, which he did often, using short paragraphs. Amy's style is similar to that of Nietzsche, in the sense that her body of work consists of bits, sketches, pieces, chapters and tweets that deal with a wide range of different issues and topics. In *The Gay Science,* he suspects that "perhaps truth is a woman who has grounds for not showing her grounds?"

One of the primary reasons a person might have for not revealing themselves is that it is terribly difficult, in the sense that figuring out who you are often requires a radical critique of your sense of self. There is the person that others see, and there is the person that perhaps you want to be, but when you try to figure out who you are, you are calling both of these into question. When Nietzsche describes humanity as being like a person who is suspended, like a tightrope over a great chasm, staring downward into the abyss, he is articulating the difficulties associated with figuring out one's identity—the difficulties associated with figuring out who and what one is (Friedrich Nietzsche, *Thus Spoke Zarathustra*, part 1, section 4).

When you start searching for yourself, there are no easy answers, not from your friends, not from your audience, not from your enemies, not even from your reflected image in the mirror. When you search for your own identity, you start off by having to look into the nothingness of the abyss, or the nothingness of a darkened theatre as seen from the perspective of a lone comedian on the brightly-lit stage.

And it is not like you just search for your identity once, for the sake of one quip. When you search for your identity, you always seem to be doing it, and the question of who you are keeps coming back, interrupting what you are doing, and framing every one of your actions and thoughts (like the music between the skits on *Inside Amy Schumer*). Nietzsche knew the stakes involved with the search for identity. He illustrated the difficulties of finding one's own identity with his famous (and, perhaps most frightening) test of "eternal recurrence." In a hypothetical scenario, Nietzsche evokes the idea that the universe—and every single human being therein—will continue to recur throughout eternity, over and over again. He writes about this in *The Gay Science*. (Isn't that a book title Amy would have approved right away?). Nietzsche explains:

> What if some day or night a demon were to steal after you into your loneliest loneliness and say to you: "This life as you now live it and have lived it you will have to live once again and innumerable times again; and there will be nothing new in it, but every pain and every joy and every thought and sigh and everything unspeakably small or great in your life must return to you, all in the same succession and sequence . . ." Would you not throw yourself down and gnash your teeth and curse the demon who spoke thus? (*The Gay Science,* section 341)

Although I claim that Schumer and Nietzsche have some fundamental commonalities, there is definitely a vast difference in *tone*. Reading the above passage, Amy would probably respond, "Friedrich, keep it real, man. That's some dark stuff you're throwing at us here." But Nietzsche's and Schumer's processes of self-realization are significantly similar.

When searching for yourself, and finding out that every experience, every attempt to find an answer will be repeated again, and again, and again, life might seem sort of bleak. How can you live in a universe where the very questioning of your own identity will be repeated eternally? What can you do, in these situations, except to say "Fuck it, let's do some living," and accept whatever happens to you? (A very Amy-like response.)

In Nietzsche's scenario, even if you try to deny your identity, and the whole search for your identity by killing yourself, you'll just repeat this action eternally—a death repeated forever—so it really doesn't seem like there's any sense in the action. It's like being trapped in life. When you are condemned to repeating a cycle, and there is no way out of the cycle, then there is really nothing to do except to accept the cycle. When we assume that there is an eternal return of everything we have and will ever have experienced, then our most reasonable answer would ultimately be to affirm life. And Amy does just that.

For Nietzsche, that means not just accepting this life (and the identical lives we will live throughout eternity), but to fully embrace this existence. He calls it *amor fati*, meaning the love of fate. In short, say "Yes" to your life. Amy Schumer, more than any other comic that I can think of, says "Yes" to life. She embraces life and encourages each of us to embrace our lives. She is the living comedy proof of Nietzsche's concepts, because she creates herself on stage and on screen while reflecting upon herself in quite honest ways.

Amy sometimes tells us stories about losing every last spark of grace. It takes a special kind of courage to approach your own biography by relating the moments when you looked like something less than a cultural icon. In drawing on her embarrassing moments, she's able to create great comedy and thoughtful reflections on modern society as a whole. But most of all, she reassures herself that she is just fine not despite, but *because of* her imperfections; she is who she is because of her characteristics. "Love yourself!" She writes, "Your power comes from who you are and what you do!" (*The Girl with the Lower Back Tattoo,* p. 142) In this credo lies an ultimate love of life. If there actually were a demon with this dark message (Nietzsche's demon, that is), then the best you can do is not to deny the inevitable but to embrace it. This is not easy—especially when we remember that we all have our personal (metaphorical) demons to fight.

In *The Leather Special*, Amy analyses paparazzi photos of her walking around New York City with coffee as if she were one of the Kardashian sisters, even though she looked like the complete opposite of them. In these images, she appears as a "homeless person." In one picture, Amy and her sister look like they're "moving and ran out of bags." When Amy starts talking about these pictures, she suddenly switches the perspective, in the sense that she becomes a commentator on the photos instead of just their subject. In doing so, she takes back control, and she changes the unbalanced game of tabloids. By using the photos in her book and in her stand-up show, Amy is doing something marvelous; she is wresting back her identity from those who attempt to determine for her who she is. It's truly an inspiring way to create your own identity—your own self-narrative—that happens to be quite like what Nietzsche had in mind.

While it's always necessary to have some sense of self, and while it's certainly good to try to figure out who you are, Nietzsche points out that it is even better to engage in the search for identity—"in its strength and in its weakness"—as though you were trying to create a great work of art. Nietzsche tells us that when we try to create our own stories of ourselves, we should try to do it with style (*The Gay Science*, Book 4, Section 290). Amy Schumer's particular "style" is seen in the hilarious, often critical assertion of her identity, where she celebrates all the aspects of her that narrow-minded non-Nietzscheans would mistakenly call "flaws."

Amy invented herself as a comedy *persona* who is *The Girl with the Lower Back Tattoo*, the protagonist and titular character of *Trainwreck*, or the subject of those paparazzi photos that she projects on the big screen during her own show. Amy takes the offensive remarks that critics make and defines her own identity. "I wear my mistakes like badges of honor, and I celebrate them," she writes (p. 310). In this way, Amy defines herself with style, as a person who is fully aware of who she is and what she does, and who (most importantly) is totally fine with all of it.

Let Irony Rule Your Life

In her comedy, Amy spends a lot of time talking in a very specific way about sex, body issues, food, and Bradley Cooper. Her discussions are often controversial, drastic, sharp and hilariously on point.

Amy uses a style of comedy which involves an ironic sort of detachment from society. It is like Amy is taking a step back from the events of the world and criticizing what's going on. This ironic stance to the world involves a sort of skepticism, in the sense that Amy seems really to doubt whether society is doing things right. She raises some relevant questions: How are we dating? When is it a woman's last fuckable day? What's a thigh gap? Whoever might think that there are definite answers to those questions underestimates the power of society.

Richard Rorty (1931–2007) identifies this sort of skepticism as an awareness of "contingency" (really just a fancy word for the idea that everything could be completely different, or change abruptly, for anyone at any time). Contingency means that nothing is safe or definitive. A contingent world is one where everything is up for grabs, and where everything could all go to hell in a moment. Contingency is what defines a world in which someone can be famous one day and a pariah the next, a world in which trends come and go, and nothing seems to have any sort of stability.

In a contingent world, fashion or body standards, for example, are constantly up for debate. In a contingent world, no one can really agree on any sort of objective truth to anything. Sound familiar? The contingent world is just like our own, and Amy's ironic humor is one of the best ways to deal with it. Ignoring the possibility of contingency, however, allows most people to get a set of communicative beliefs and to establish, as Rorty calls it, a "final vocabulary." Rorty is skeptical about the consistency of such a "final vocabulary" and brings in an ironist, who reminds us in several respects of Amy Schumer.

When, like Amy Schumer, you spend most of your comic career gleefully poking holes in the logics that seem to define the world, you are being an ironist. In *Contingency, Irony, and Solidarity*, Rorty characterizes the ironist as a person who is

> never quite able to take themselves seriously because always aware that the terms in which they describe themselves are subject to change, always aware of the contingency and fragility of their final vocabularies, and thus of their selves. (p. 74)

Amy, similarly (like most good comics) tends to burn all of her material once in a while and start back at square one. In destroying her material, Amy is literally destroying any chance she has of adopting a final vocabulary. Because a lot of her comedic material tends to be a creation of her own identity in reference to society, Amy is recreating herself and her criticism of society every time she creates new material.

Amy has literally no "final vocabulary," in the sense Rorty describes. She creates herself over and over again on stage and in her sketches. There is always new material. An Amy Schumer show is unique and incomparable, every time. Amy takes concrete steps to create herself and criticizes society by never adopting a final vocabulary. The result is brilliant comedy that is a profound creation of the self and potent social criticism at once.

To create great and insightful comedy, you can't take yourself too seriously. You need to think outside of the box to realize what is going on around you. You need to think like a stranger in your own society. That's exactly what Amy does, just like Rorty's ironist:

> The ironist spends her time worrying about the possibility that she has been initiated into the wrong tribe, taught to play the wrong language game. She worries that the process of socialization which turned her into a human being by giving her a language may have given her the wrong language, and so turned her into the wrong kind of human being. (p. 75)

That's why the ironist is always suspicious about someone's "final vocabulary," including her own. So how does an ironist figure out if she is the right kind of human being? Is it like trying to figure out whether a joke is actually funny? The way to answer that question is by talking to other people—by getting some sense of who they are and what they are up to. Rorty tells us that the ironist's (or ironic comedian's) doubts about themselves and the world can only be assuaged by getting to know others.

So we get a microphone and go to the streets to interview people, or we invite them into a casual atmosphere to discuss aspects of their unfamiliar lives. On *Inside Amy Schumer*, there's a segment called "Amy Goes Deep," in which Amy does exactly what Rorty suggests. She meets people she wouldn't otherwise meet on a regular basis, which in turn broadens both her and the audience's minds. This corresponds to what Richard Rorty describes as the "post-philosophical" culture, where no philosopher is better than a poet or a writer. Everyone can give profound insights and competent thoughts about our culture, and that is exactly what Amy does with her comedy.

Emerging Amy, the Comedian Self

It's one thing to be yourself and another to become what you eventually can embrace. This is where other human beings become an essential part of who we eventually are. In addition to being a Nietzschean who defies the concept of a final vocabulary, Amy Schumer is also a great example of the theory of symbolic interactionism, described by the underrated American philosopher George Herbert Mead (1863–1931).

Mead's work focused on the development of the self, which is why he is today recognized as one of the founders of social psychology. It's notable that Mead did not publish any books in his long career. It was not until his death that several of his students put together and edited some volumes from his lecture notes at the University of Chicago. The most famous of those volumes is *Mind, Self, and Society* (1934), where Mead develops the appealing theory that our mind arises out of the social act of communication. He claims that the individual mind is nothing without the relation to other minds and their shared meanings. In other words, we all came to be in the first place through the social process of communication.

Mead explains all of this in a complex approach of symbolic behaviour, social actions, linguistic behaviour, role taking, and the social interplay of individuals. In short, according to Mead, the self is the result of a social process, due to communication between what he calls the "I" (the pure form of self, independent of a social process) and the "Me" (the self determined by a social process). In this process, the so-called "significant other"—mostly, our family members—helps us to learn things within our social environment.

Even our negative experiences contribute to the social formation of a self. That's to say, there are good and bad influences on "Me." Many of Amy's stories (and jokes) come out of bad experiences in her past. These are often situations in which Amy met dickheads or received negative responses for being a woman who makes people laugh. Whether it's a past sociopathic restaurant manager or a nasty online troll, nowadays, the bad role models in Amy's life eventually lead her to do good things.

To get through life, Amy made people laugh. Amy remembers: "Whether it was teachers catching me talking in class or cops catching me with beer in my backpack on the beach, it always felt like my only way to get home free was to make everyone laugh," she writes. "It always dismantled the power structure within seconds. Being funny was my ultimate hustle!" (p. 100).

She found her way to herself through others by taking on the critics and transforming their words into something profoundly personal and funny at the same time. In part, Amy became who she now is because of the people who rejected and dismissed her. By remembering her critics, Amy took their judgements and put them to her advantage.

And now, she is known for being successful at what she loves with a body of work that is honest, hard-earned and most of all, utterly inspiring.

6
No Wisdom to Offer You

JERED JANES

In a 2015 piece for *The Atlantic*, Megan Garber suggests that comedians have recently begun to play the role of public intellectuals. (Her article is titled, "How Comedians Became Public Intellectuals".) Garber presents Amy Schumer as one example of such a comedian.

According to Garber, Schumer and other comedians play this role because, in addition to reaching large audiences, "they're exploring and wrestling with important ideas. They're sharing their conclusions with the rest of us. They're providing fodder for discussion, not just of the minutiae of everyday experience, but of the biggest questions of the day." Garber cites the *Inside Amy Schumer* sketch "Court of Public Opinion: The Trial of Bill Cosby" as an example.

A few days later, Elizabeth Bruenig published a response to Garber. (Her article is titled, "Comedians Are Funny, Not Public Intellectuals".) Bruenig points out that comedians like Schumer are ultimately entertainers, that "entertainers . . . . rely on mass adulation to remain gainfully employed," and that this means that comedians "have a special motivation to flatter their audiences."

Bruenig notes that flattering audiences requires comedians to do two things. First, comedians must affirm the audience's "pre-conceived notions about morality and politics." Second, they must "linger in the radical center." This means that two things comedians *don't do* are 1. challenge audiences' moral and political prejudices; and 2. show them genuinely radical political alternatives.

These are precisely the kinds of things that public intellectuals are supposed to do, the things that comedians don't. Public intellectuals are not merely supposed to tackle the most important questions of their time and convey their own views on these questions to large audiences. They're supposed to do these things from as *radical* of a political perspective as they think required and *without regard* for whether their contributions will flatter their audiences. Because she thinks comedians don't do these two things, Bruenig concludes that, if comedians like Schumer are now our public intellectuals, we're worse off for it.

Garber's and Bruenig's articles raise a deceptively simple and important question: Do comedians now play the role of public intellectuals? Given Schumer's prominence in Garber's article—even the photo accompanying it is of a cape-clad Schumer levitating over the MTV Movie Awards stage in 2015—and her position as one of the most influential and thought-provoking comedians around, it's worth considering: Is Amy Schumer a public intellectual?

Public Intellectuals

Public intellectuals are people who, according to Garber, tackle "the biggest questions of the day." They are people who, according to Bruenig, consider these questions from as radical a perspective as they think required and without regard for whether anyone or any institution will be flattered by their answers. And they are people who share these answers with the public, sometimes along with their thought processes and the reasons that justify their answers. Sharing these processes and these justificatory reasons is not always possible. because it's not always possible to convey to the public the wealth of knowledge and the complexity of thought that public intellectuals employ in considering these questions and in reaching these answers.

The job of public intellectuals is thus not to explain to the public *all* of the reasons behind their answers to the biggest questions of the day. The public intellectual doesn't have to equip the public with the tools necessary to think through these questions for themselves and to come to their own conclusions on the basis of their own justificatory reasons. Their job is to use their exceptional skills to consider these questions without regard for how their answers will be received and to share these answers with the public.

Consider, for example, Noam Chomsky. Since the 1960s, Chomsky has been widely regarded as a leading public intellectual for providing critical views on the most pressing issues in American politics, and in particular, American foreign policy. While Chomsky publishes books in which he articulates his views and explains his reasons for holding them, this isn't what makes him a public intellectual. What makes him a public intellectual is that he articulates his views on the biggest questions of the day to the public through media like television and YouTube, and through easier to digest forms of communication like interviews. In doing so, Chomsky doesn't focus on explaining to the public precisely *why* he holds the views he does. He doesn't focus on providing the public with the tools necessary to think through the issues themselves and to come to their own conclusions on the basis of their own justificatory reasons. Instead, he focuses on thinking through the issues himself and conveying his conclusions to the public.

Philosophers, Public Philosophers, and Public Intellectuals

Consider Socrates, as he is revealed in Plato's dialogues. (Socrates never wrote anything himself; what we know of him is from how he is conveyed by other philosophers, primarily Plato.) The fifth-century B.C.E. Greek philosopher was widely known among his contemporary Athenians. He devoted substantial amounts of time to talking in public settings with fellow Athenians about the most important questions and issues facing human beings.

According to a traditional view, a philosopher is someone who engages the most important questions and issues facing human beings and who, crucially, aims to develop her own positions on them on the basis of her own justificatory reasons. Socrates was certainly a philosopher in this sense: he certainly had his own views on the questions and issues he discussed with others, views that he endorsed on the basis of his own justificatory reasons. In fact, this traditional view of the philosopher probably has its origin with Socrates and Plato.

But in Plato's dialogues, the Socrates we encounter is not primarily concerned with relaying *his* views of these things to his audience. His primary concern was to question his audience about *their* views of these things and *their* reasons for endorsing these views. In doing so, Socrates's aim wasn't to show that these views and justificatory reasons are deficient and that the audience should therefore defer to him when it comes to the most important questions and issues facing human beings. Instead, it was to help his audience develop *their own* views on the basis of *their own* justificatory reasons. It's for this reason that Socrates was not merely a philosopher but also a *public philosopher*.

There are thus essential differences between public intellectuals, philosophers, and public philosophers. Public intellectuals use their exceptional skills to consider the biggest questions of the day, to come to their own conclusions regarding them on the basis of their own justificatory reasons, and to share these conclusions with the public. For example, Chomsky considered whether the contemporary Antifa movement is an effective way to combat fascism, and he concluded on the basis of his own reasons that it's not. Furthermore, he recently shared this conclusion with the public through a widely read newspaper. Philosophers consider the most important questions and issues facing human beings and come to their own conclusions on these things on the basis of their own justificatory reasons. Plato, for example, wondered what the difference between knowing something and merely believing something is, and he concluded on the basis of his own justificatory reasons that knowing something involves having not merely a belief but a true belief that one can justify. Finally, public philosophers help their audiences to consider the most important questions and issues facing human beings and to develop their own views on them on the basis of their own justificatory reasons.

In short, this means that whereas a public intellectual makes sense of the biggest questions of the day *for the public* on the basis of *her* justificatory reasons, and whereas a philosopher makes sense of the most important questions and issues facing human beings *for herself* on the basis of *her* justificatory reasons, public philosophers help the public make sense of these questions and issues *for themselves* on the basis of *their* own justificatory reasons.

To claim, as Garber does, that Schumer is one of today's public intellectuals is thus to claim that she considers the biggest questions of the day, reaches her own conclusions on them on the basis of her own justificatory reasons, and then shares these conclusions with the public with a view to making sense of these questions for the public. It's to claim that in, for example, the *Inside Amy Schumer* sketch "Girl, You Don't Need Makeup," Schumer not only has thought about the mixed messages women get regarding the use of makeup and has come to her own conclusions about these messages, but that she somehow also expresses to her audience, through this sketch, an unambiguous and easily appropriated conclusion regarding these messages.

No Wisdom to Offer?

The first problem with the idea that Amy Schumer is a public intellectual is that Schumer herself claims that she has no wisdom to offer us. Because comedians often assume the role of a character that's based on, but ultimately distinct from themselves, it's difficult to tell when they're conveying their own views on an issue. For this reason, figuring out how Schumer understands herself and her work on the basis of her standup, TV shows, movies, and even interviews, is a bit tricky. Fortunately, her autobiography offers more of a direct line into her own views.

In "A Note to My Readers," a note which opens *The Girl with the Lower Back Tattoo*, Schumer writes: "I'm a flawed fuckup and I haven't figured anything out, so I have no wisdom to offer you. But what I *can* help with is showing you my mistakes and my pain and my laughter" (p. 2). These aren't the words of a comedian who understands her work to consist of sharing her conclusions on the biggest questions of the day with the public. In other words, they're not the words of a comedian who conceives of herself as a public intellectual.

They're the words of a comedian who understands her work to be a source of practical insight and laughter-induced solace for her audience. In fact, Schumer here almost explicitly warns us against regarding her as a public intellectual! Of course, so did Socrates. As Plato reports in a dialogue conveying Socrates's trial for heresy and corrupting the youth (*Apology*), "He, O men, is the wisest, who, like Socrates, knows that his wisdom is in truth worth nothing."

Schumer doesn't need to understand herself as a public intellectual in order to be one. She could, after all, have the impact of a public intellectual without intending to or without even realizing it. Undoubtedly, Garber thinks this is the case. But—and this is the second problem with the idea that Schumer is a public intellectual—to think this is to miss the unique function of comedy in general, and Schumer's comedy in particular.

Unlike public intellectuals, comedians like Schumer don't make sense of the day's biggest questions *for* the public. They don't present their audiences with clear and easily appropriated answers to these questions. Instead, they challenge their audiences to make sense of the questions *for themselves* on the basis of *their own* justificatory reasons. Comedy is an exceptionally engaging and uniquely effective way to help people do this. In other words, through her comedic work, Amy Schumer is not a public intellectual (as Garber proposes); she's a public philosopher.

Football Town Nights

To see just how Schumer plays the role of public philosopher, let's consider two sketches from *Inside Amy Schumer*. The first of these sketches is "Football Town Nights," a spoof of the popular *Friday Night Lights*. Here Schumer (and company) confronts us with the Bronconeers, a high-school football team with a new coach. He demands at the outset of the season that, in addition to running a no-huddle offense and practicing twice a day, players refrain from *raping*. After fielding numerous ridiculous but, in some cases, unfortunately plausible questions from the players ("What if my mom is the DA, and won't prosecute, can I rape?"; "What if the girl said yes to me the other day, but it was about something else?"; or "What if the girl said yes, but then she changes her mind out of nowhere, like a crazy person?") and from community members ("How are our boys supposed to celebrate when they win? Or blow off steam when they lose?"), the coach finds his team down by fifteen points at halftime, at least in part because his players are distracted by thoughts of the newly forbidden rapes.

Frustrated by their misplaced focus and their ostensible misunderstanding of what football is all about, the coach berates them in the locker room. "How do I get through to you boys that football isn't about rape?" he begins. He immediately continues: "It's about violently dominating anyone that stands between you and what you want. Now you gotta get yourself into the mindset that you are gods, and you are entitled to this. That other team, they ain't just gonna lay down and give it to you. You gotta go out there and take it."

The tension between the coach's plausible first line—"football isn't about rape!"—and the equally plausible lines that follow it force the audience to consider the relationship between football culture and rape culture. More specifically, it forces us to consider how the environment in which football is practiced and played, an environment where a sense of entitlement and a willingness to be violent are assets, may directly contribute to an environment in which women's bodies are viewed as objects for men's taking and in which rape doesn't merely occur but does so with astounding frequency.

A public intellectual could certainly give a speech about the connection or lack thereof between football culture and rape culture, a speech in which she explains to the public her conclusions, formed on the basis of her own justificatory reasons about the issue. And of course Schumer herself could take time out of her standup, TV show, movies and books, to do the same. Crucially, she doesn't. She instead gives us this hilarious sketch—with, among other things, a caricatured Tami Taylor who drinks (and spills) wine out of an increasingly and ridiculously large wine glass—and this unexpected and trenchant final scene.

Schumer doesn't present to the audience the conclusions she's reached on the basis of her own justificatory reasons about the connection between football culture and rape culture. Instead, she puts the audience in the position of laughing their way into a final scene where it's nearly impossible not to at least *consider* whether there's a connection between these two cultures (and what that connection might be). In other words, she invites the audience to begin considering for themselves whether, and what, this connection might be, and she provides some resources with which this consideration might be carried out (insights and tacitly posed questions).

Is there a connection between the aggression and violence essential to successful football and the aggression and violence present in rape culture? Do we send boys and young men involved in football mixed messages about the kinds of people they should be? In this way, Schumer functions not as a public intellectual but as a public philosopher, one who encourages her audience to consider important questions and come to their own conclusions on the basis of their own justificatory reasons.

The Trial of Bill Cosby

"Court of Public Opinion: The Trial of Bill Cosby" opens as Bill Cosby's defense attorney, played by Schumer, begins her closing argument. In the course of her hilariously absurd comments, the lawyer attempts through various means (dancing to the theme song to *The Cosby Show*, equating Cosby with Cliff Huxtable, and providing the jury with their own pudding pops and Cosby sweaters) to shift the jury's attention from whether or not Cosby committed any crimes to whether or not fans of his work, like themselves, deserve to enjoy his work.

"Let's remind ourselves what's at stake here," she says. "If convicted, the next time you put on a rerun of *The Cosby Show*, you may wince a little. You might feel a little pang. And none of us deserve that. We don't deserve to feel that pang. We deserve to dance like no one's watching. And watch like no one's raping."

The sketch forces the audience to consider the role of public opinion in the criminal justice system and whether we value our own un-conflicted entertainment over justice. Again, a public intellectual could certainly give a speech in which she explains to the public her conclusions (formed on the basis of her own justificatory reasons) concerning these issues. And, again, of course Schumer could take the time to give that speech. But she doesn't, opting instead to present a ridiculous and funny sketch that evokes the audience's positive associations with the Huxtables and Cosby while at the same time pointing out that such associations might be dangerous.

Again, Schumer doesn't present to the audience the conclusions she's reached on the basis of her own justificatory reasons about the influence of public opinion on justice and our desire for un-conflicted entertainment. Instead, she puts the audience in the position of laughing their way through a sketch that makes it nearly impossible not to at least consider the idea that perhaps our judgments of cases are swayed by the absurd fact that we don't want to feel guilty watching *The Cosby Show.* Is it wrong to pretend people aren't getting raped so that I can watch reruns in peace? Schumer demands we ask this question. In other words, she invites the audience to begin considering whether public opinion influences the criminal justice system and if so how, and whether they value their own un-conflicted entertainment over justice. Again, in this way, Schumer doesn't function as a public intellectual but as a public philosopher.

How Comedians Became Public Philosophers

Laughing isn't something we *do* as much as something that happens *to* us or *through* us. It's not something we schedule and consciously initiate; it's something that overtakes us in its own time. This can happen without our conscious consent, as when we think we're in no mood to laugh but find ourselves nevertheless laughing. But it can also happen entirely despite ourselves, as when we try but fail to restrain laughter at something we know we shouldn't laugh at. Sometimes we find ourselves laughing before we realize it, for reasons we don't understand. "Why was that so funny?" we might ask ourselves.

Comedy is the attempt to induce laughter in people, and those who undertake this attempt (we call them "comedians") are accordingly powerful people: their skills allow them to induce states of laughter in their audiences, states over which their audiences may have little or no control and concerning which they may have little or no initial understanding. The ability of comedy and comedians to operate on us in ways that outpace our control and understanding is part of what makes comedy and comedians so interesting and important, and part of what gives them a power that no essayist, treatise writer, philosopher, or public intellectual can have.

It's also what makes comedians in general and Amy Schumer in particular such effective public philosophers. By causing laughter to arise in us regarding the possible connection between football culture and rape culture, or the role of public opinion in the criminal justice system, or the relationship between justice and our desire for un-conflicted entertainment, Schumer doesn't fill our minds with her convictions. Instead, often unbeknownst to us and despite ourselves, she prepares the ground for us to consider what our own convictions on these important matters should be.

7
Amy Schumer or the Incongruities

NOËL CARROLL

Amy Schumer's sketch-comedy routine "Boner Doctor" from Comedy Central's *Inside Amy Schumer* opens with what looks like a genuine advertisement for a drug-treatment for erectile dysfunction. As the customary warning, "If you have an erection for more than four hours . . ." begins, it is suddenly interrupted by "Doctor" Amy Schumer, who excitedly interjects a perky, "Call me!"

She then suggests an alternative procedure to the problem than the typically recommended medical one. Among other things, she promises, "If I can't wrestle that gator down, no doctor will be able to." It soon becomes evident that, despite her white lab coat, Amy Schumer is no doctor, but what she might describe in one of her routines as "a horny chick." She coyly confides that her treatment is free, is available at any time of day and that the phone number on the screen is hers. This faux advertisement is basically a ruse to, so to speak, get her hands on some reliable loving which, if not endless, will be protracted.

The prospective patient's persisting erection is not treated as an affliction, but as an opportunity—at least for Dr. Schumer, who has spent the last three New Year's Eves sex-starved. Moreover, should you have any doubts about Dr. Schumer's AMA approval rating (or lack thereof), she strips off her lab coat early on, gloating about how easy it is to get one, and revealing underneath a form-fitting, short red dress.

The underlying humor of the routine is that what advertises itself as a cure is really a thinly guised plot for Dr. Schumer to have as much sex as possible (or at least some). Like a pun, the sketch has two meanings, and the tension between them (the lofty Hippocratic one versus its down and dirty double) is the source of our comic amusement.

The character of Dr. Schumer here is very consistent with the persona that Amy Schumer projects throughout her oeuvre. In her "Just for Laughs" concert in Montreal, she whispers sheepishly, but also while beaming with pride, that "I'm slutty"; and in her "Ballerina Erotica,"while interviewing a lap dancer, she asserts "I would bet I'm a bigger whore than you are." In addition, she feigns wonderment when learning how much money a lap dancer can make, since "I have done it so many times for free." And her film *Trainwreck* (in which she not only stars but which she also wrote) revels for comic effect in her careless amorous adventures.

Nor is it only the sexual id that Amy Schumer embodies. She is appetite incarnate. She piles food into her mouth with abandon and imbibes alcohol of every variety, in every combination, and in vast amounts. Rabelais (the Renaissance master of ribald tales and songs) would have loved her.

Because Schumer's comedy is so often concerned with excessive carnal desires, it may seem that the best philosophical framework for explicating it would be that of psychoanalysis. However, in this essay, I will challenge that presumption, arguing that the incongruity theory of comic amusement is a better philosophical option for getting at the nature of Amy Schumer's achievement.

In order to demonstrate this, I will outline Freud's theory of wit, its putative relevance to Amy Schumer's comedy, and the shortcomings of psychoanalysis in that regard. Then we'll need a description of the incongruity theory of comic amusement—the theory that probably is the one most commonly endorsed by contemporary philosophers and psychologists. In my opinion, the application of incongruity theory to Amy Schumer's comedy demonstrates its superiority to the psychoanalytic approach.

The Psychoanalytic Theory of Wit

Undoubtedly, the *locus classicus* of the psychoanalytic theory of humor is Sigmund Freud's *Wit and its Relation to the Unconscious.* On Freud's account of humor, there are two different kinds of wit: harmless wit, as exemplified by nonsense jests (for example, "What do you call the grape that conquered the world?" "Alexander the Grape"); and more content-full humor, where the content is typically of a hostile or obscene sort, and which we may call "tendentious" wit (a joke with a point). Moreover, these two types of wit are most frequently related functionally.

For Freud, the "I" or ego must negotiate between the id or libido, the source of desire and raw emotion, and the superego, the source of morality (characteristically highly censorious). In the ordinary course of things, the superego, in a manner of speaking, functions as a defense against immoral, hostile, obscene, and sexual impulses. Generally, the superego would punish the ego with lacerating guilt for flirting with unseemly sexual material, such as regarding a four-hour erection as an opportunity for fun and games. And yet it seems irrefutable that we are able to derive pleasure from the lascivious routines in which Amy Schumer specializes, not to mention the whole vast repertoire of what we call "dirty jokes."

Given the superego, how is this possible?

This is where harmless wit comes into play for the psychoanalyst. Basically harmless humor (nonsense) disguises or masks the tendentious content of routines, like Amy Schumer's, in a way that enables it to slip past the censorious superego which, beguiled by silliness, relaxes its vigilance, so that we can momentarily enjoy the sexual content that Amy Schumer purveys, affording a surprised jolt of pleasure that manifests itself in laughter.

In "Boner Doctor," Schumer's obvious pretense of being a doctor—a bit of silly make-believe, made all the more nonsensical for being so (intentionally) clumsily transparent—provides a screen of absurdity that enables Schumer to smuggle her seemingly insatiable sexual desires past the censor, thereby allowing us to indulge our usually forbidden fantasies. That is, Schumer's childlike pretend play (making believe she's a doctor) neutralizes the censor, thereby titillating our ids, whereas an open and direct expression of sexuality, unmediated by the playful pretense, would be immediately squashed by the super-ego.

In addition to making the psyche seem like a community of little beings (the homunculi: ego, id, and superego), the psychoanalytic theorist employs a hydraulic analogy with even further metaphysical commitments. The id, home of libidinal desire, is pent up with the energy of hidden wishes in search of release. This energy is like rising water in search of an outlet, like the sluice of a lock gate in a canal or dam. The harmless wit of a sketch like "Boner Doctor" secures a momentary relaxation of the repressive grip of the superego, thereby opening the sluice and facilitating the outpouring of some of the id's heretofore suppressed desires in the process of our exposure to the tendentious dimensions of the wit. The superego, tricked by the harmless wit, lifts its resistance to the sketch, allowing for a feeling of release.

There are unquestionably many problems with the tripartite theory of the psyche and the hydraulic conception of its operation (the pent-up water within a dam) that are presupposed by the psychoanalytic theory of wit. However, rather than attack the very foundations of psychoanalytic theory, a project too large for a brief essay such as this, let us put these problems aside for the moment and ask how well, on its own terms, does psychoanalysis account for Amy Schumer's humor?

One problem, it seems to me, is that, supposing there is such an entity as the superego, the theory makes it appear utterly benighted (that is, naïve, ignorant, or "in the dark"). For all its vaunted vigilance, it is rather easily duped. It is slower on the uptake than the most obtuse straight-man in the broadest of comedy routines. Moreover, once Schumer gets her first off-color laugh, why doesn't the superego shut the whole thing down, leaving us shuddering with guilt? Why does it allow us to continue to watch? How can it keep falling for the disguise of the harmless wit?

Indeed, how did it fall for it in the first place? Didn't it realize that we were tuning into *Inside Amy Schumer* and what that entailed? The psychoanalytic theory of wit assumes that the superego is surprised or tricked into permitting our exposure to the repressed, tendentious component of the wit. But for this assumption to obtain, it requires that the superego must be monumentally blind to a stunning amount of information that is readily available to a mind of moderate intelligence. Why is the censor (!) so dim*witted*?

Indeed, the psychoanalytic account rests on the notion of hidden desires being suddenly made public. But given how pervasive stimulus is in contemporary society, it is difficult to imagine any adult being surprised by sex. As Foucault pointed out in the first volume of his *History of Sexuality*, there has never been as much discussion of sexuality as since Freud's discovery of repression.

These, of course, are objections that obtain across the board to the psychoanalytic account of "dirty jokes" in general. But the account, in treating Amy Schumer's comedy as run-of-the-mill off-color humor, does not do justice to Schumer's ambition which, for want of a better word, we might call its *feminism*. In order to explain this aspect of Schumer's humor and to appreciate it in a way that the psychoanalytic account does not, let us now turn to the incongruity theory of comic amusement.

The Incongruity Theory of Comic Amusement

The incongruity theory of comic amusement maintains that the source of comic amusement is the perception of incongruity. "Incongruity" presupposes a contrast with "congruity," which, for our purposes, we shall understand as "our expectations about the way things are or should be." Incongruities involve the violation of norms—norms of logic, of physics, of all the sciences and morality, of law, probability, etiquette, hygiene, good taste, grammar, semantics, sexuality, sportsmanship, stereotypes, social scripts and schemas, heuristics, and you-name-it. In jest, dogs talk, angels gossip, and priests, ministers, and rabbis seem to always congregate in groups.

For a concrete example of humor:

> A priest is walking downtown when a prostitute comes up to him and says, "$25 will get you a blow job, padre." Perplexed, the priest returns to the rectory and upon seeing Sister Catherine, he asks: "What's a blow-job?" to which Sister Catherine replies, "$25, same as downtown."

Here the punchline is incongruous, since this is not how we think nuns are or should be.

In an early scene in the movie *Trainwreck*, the father attempts to explain to his two daughters why he and their mother are separating. He uses an analogy with dolls to rationalize his infidelity, asking them how they would feel if they could only play with one doll and not others, including with their friends' dolls, and so on. A large part of the absurdity here has to do with a deep conceptual confusion, namely, that dolls are objects, not persons, and it is not ethically virtuous to treat people, such as one's wife, as objects. That is, the father inappropriately (or incongruously) subsumes dolls under the concept of persons. Of course, another part of the humor also has to do with the slyness of the analogy the father uses to mislead his hapless daughters. But that too is a moral violation. It is not the way things should be. Fathers should not deceive their guileless daughters, perhaps especially about deceiving their wives.

Of course, not all incongruities are comically amusing. Some are frightening. If a caregiver makes a funny face, a child is apt to laugh, but if a stranger does the same, the child may cry. In order to be comically amusing, the incongruity must not be anxiety producing.

Likewise, inasmuch as incongruities are puzzling, they may elicit a problem-solving response. One might be tempted to try to explain an encounter with a deviation from our expectations of how things are or should be. Given the surprise election of President Trump, pundits have been at pains to explain how it happened.

But that is not the way with comic incongruities like saucy Sister Catherine. If initially taken aback by her response to the priest, we nevertheless do not go on to try to make sense of it. We relax and enjoy it as nonsense. Where the incongruity elicits anxiety or poses a cognitive challenge, we ready ourselves to respond. But in the case of comic amusement, we recognize the absurdity for what it is and, so to say, stand down. Our relief registers to us as a feeling of levity.

Summarizing formally, something is an instance of comic amusement just in case 1. its object is a perceived incongruity, which is 2. not anxiety producing, and which is 3. not a genuine cognitive challenge, but whose 4. recognized absurdity 5. elicits a feeling of levity, which is 6. enjoyed. Whether or not this definition succeeds as an essential or exceptionless account of comic amusement, I nevertheless recommend it as the most serviceable heuristic we have for analyzing the phenomenon. In other words, given a specimen of humor, look for the evidence of non-threatening, cognitively non-challenging incongruities, and you will be on your way to isolating the comic levers at play in the situation. In other words, try it, you'll like it. Also note that the incongruity is "perceived." That is, the object of comic amusement may not be incongruous, but is perceived as such. Moreover, the object of comic amusement—the perceived incongruity—is what we generally call "humor."

When we apply the incongruity theory to the humor of Amy Schumer, we observe a very frequently recurring theme, namely, that of the consistent subversion of the prevailing stereotypes of "ladylike" deportment and the social scripts of feminine behavior. Whereas women are supposedly the modest gender, Schumer aggressively celebrates immodesty. Schumer flagrantly disputes the social myth that women are not interested in sex. She makes the Wife of Bath (from Chaucer's *The Canterbury Tales*) look like an amateur. Amy Schumer, a.k.a. the

Boner Doctor, pursues sex, as society would have it, as men do. Much of her humor has to do specifically with this role reversal. But she wears her Scarlet Letter with pride.

Similarly, Schumer's immoderate eating and drinking are also "unbecoming" for a woman. Not only does she binge drink and overeat, but she does it with the indelicacy of a fraternity jock on party night. (I highlight her out of place demand for curly fries in the sketch, "Love Tub" as an example.) Whereas the social script for female behavior calls for women to be neat, Amy Schumer's comic persona is—not to put too fine a point on it—a slob.

And she plays on that slovenliness. In "Sexting," we open on Amy eating pasta with her hands from a colander when she receives a text from "Bobby"; she sends him some awkward messages ("Rub all my feet") before going back to her movie. We laugh at the incongruity between her present state of messy gluttony and her attempts at sexiness. She revisits this theme in "Chicks Can Hang"; Amy rams a burger in her face, and a nearby male comments, "My boner just got a boner."

Rather than dainty and demure, she is consistently both raucous and raunchy. It is hard to think of a feminine social code that Schumer does not try to violate. She is Miss Manners—NOT!

This is what I earlier referred to as Schumer's *feminism*, which can be understood as her sustained attack on female stereotypes that portray women as sexually passive, meek, tidy, restrained, and made of sugar and spice and everything nice. By following what appear to be male behavioral scripts, Schumer evokes laughter through her incongruous transgression of social norms of female decorum. This is feminist not only in the sense that it claims the right to level the playing field between women and men, but also because it calls into question the codes of feminine propriety or correctness that are inventions that can function as social constraints.

Waving aside the various problems that the psychoanalytic theory of wit confronts, at its best, it would propose that the crux of Schumer's humor is its traffic in salacious material, its parading of hidden desires, and its sexual exhibitionism. In this, it fails to distinguish Schumer's humor from its account of any other form of off-color or "bathroom" humor. Thus, it fails to identify it as feminist humor.

On the other hand, the incongruity theory of humor not only situates Schumer's comedy in the context of a general theory of comic amusement, but the theory is also able to pinpoint its specifically feminist dimension by emphasizing the ways in which it incongruously subverts still influential conceptions of female behavior, especially with reference to the themes of desire, most notably sexual desire, and other carnal appetites. In this regard, the incongruity theory of comic amusement is a better, more exact fit for Schumer's comedy than the psychoanalytic theory of wit.

All-Told

The best approach to the comedy of Amy Schumer is a non-psychoanalytic, philosophical approach. The incongruity theory of comic amusement is superior to a Freudian account, despite the fact that the latter would appear to have a natural claim on Schumer's humor, given its sexual bent. But the psychoanalytic approach, in addition to its many general theoretical liabilities, also fails to hone in on what is specific to Schumer's comedy, namely its feminist dimension.

In contrast, this is something the incongruity theory can accommodate handily. Moreover, the incongruity theory is not only superior to the psychoanalytic theory in this case. As a general theory of comic amusement, it can subsume whatever is valuable in the psychoanalytic theory without being subject to the same failings.

The psychoanalytic theory speaks of harmless wit and tendentious wit. The incongruity theory can assimilate these in terms of incongruities of sense and incongruities of the relevant norms without appealing to a homunculi-theory of mind, a hydraulic system of libidinal energy, or the rest of the Freudian theory.

Thus the incongruity theorist can say to the psychoanalyst: anything you can do, I can do better.

8
Sexistentialism

GERALD BROWNING

The comedy of Amy Schumer, much like that of many of her contemporaries, uses absurdity as a powerful comedic device to set up a punchline.

When we hear the word "absurd", what comes to mind is something that makes no sense or is illogical. In the philosophical sense, "absurd" refers to the notion of searching for meaning in something that is meaningless. And in many cases, what is referred to as "meaningless" is life (that is to say, life has no purpose).

Schumer's work often showcases what is illogical about what goes on between men and women with regard to sex, especially in her blockbuster movie, *Trainwreck*, although the theme is common to some of her other works. By shedding some light on the total lack of logic with which we attempt to deal with the world and each other (the absurdity), Schumer offers a scathing portrayal and analysis of gender and social relations.

Albert Camus, author of *The Myth of Sisyphus*, wrote on the futility that is inherent in pursuing the meaning of life. His notion is that there is no meaning in life; thus, the quest to find meaning in life is the very definition of absurdity. It is a venture in which we constantly engage and in which we are doomed to fail. This failure is symbolized in the story of Sisyphus, condemned to eternal futility, doomed to carry a heavy rock up a hill, only to have the rock roll down the hill, so that it has to be carried up again, forever.

In her humor, Schumer shows how absurd the concept of "masculinity" can be. She critically analyzes the logic in a male-dominated society as a way to express her belief in the absurdity of masculinity and the patriarchal society in which such ideas flourish. Audiences laugh at Amy Schumer's antics in the film, all the while laughing at the sexism and idiocy of the stereotype itself. While Schumer's movie pokes fun at the male stereotype (the absurdity), her ending is completely existential—she owns the absurdity and rolls with it.

At the end of the movie, Schumer's character finds herself falling in love and committing to the boyfriend character, Dr. Aaron Conners (played by Bill Hader). It's typical of the genre for the commitment-phobe to have a sudden change of heart and embrace a more committed relationship status. The fact that this happens despite an ongoing internal critique of the genre is what makes this ending operate at another level.

We have the option of interpreting her movie as if it were just another romantic comedy. A commitment-phobe learns their lesson and commits to embracing gender stereotypes (thus the cheerleader uniform). In our search for the meaning of Schumer's brilliant movie, she gives us the option to fail. We might see it as just another comedy, having searched for meaning and failed. Or we might find the meaning in that failure. We tried to have a self-aware comedy that defied gender stereotyping, but they always end up together anyway.

Much like Camus's perception that we try to find meaning in a meaningless existence, Schumer's movie acts as a criticism of the patriarchal society, in the hopes of evoking a change that may never happen. That may sound pessimistic, but it's thoroughly existentialist.

The Battle of the Sexes

In much of Schumer's work, there is absurdity in the interactions between opposite genders as well as amongst people of the same gender. One of my favorite sketches of *Inside Amy Schumer* has to be early in the first season.

Amy is standing around out in her neighborhood with a few girlfriends. Each woman is attempting to compliment the other; however, the friends cannot accept a compliment and end up putting themselves down in horrible ways. For the women to put themselves down in such horrible ways (each put-down slightly worse and more off-color than the last) is pointless, to say the least. "I look like a whore locked out of her apartment," one says about herself. When another is congratulated for a promotion, the woman replies, "I'm going to be fired in two seconds . . . I am legally retarded."

This absurdity seems to illustrate Schumer's point of how unnecessary it is to feel that there is a competition amongst the genders. On the one hand, she points to the absurdity of how women are expected to accomplish great things but not to take credit for them. On the other hand, they're *at the same moment* engaged in a humility competition, itself an absurd concept. What is the point in topping one another's put downs? The sketch ends with another friend casually walking towards the group. She is complimented, and the new arrival actually accepts the compliment. She replies with a perky, "Thank you." The others, frustrated over this response, turn their self-hatred onto themselves in horrible acts of suicide. We even see one of them setting herself on fire! This ending seems to demand that we ask the question: "What is the worst that could happen if a woman actually accepted a compliment?" The answer Amy gives us: everyone dies.

When looking at this particular example, you can see both sorts of perceptions of the absurd. The *illogical* idea in this skit exemplifies absurdist humor; she's pointing to the fact that we think people should take credit for accomplishments but also that women shouldn't. Of course, it is over the top and ludicrous. Yet, one can also see that there is another element of the absurd at work here. Admittedly, I am looking at this from a pessimistic point of view, but I think that this joke was meant to point out that women are not only victims of the social structure (where they cannot even have enough self-esteem to accept a compliment), but they are also the perpetrators of the same social structure. No man is around policing on behalf of the patriarchy.

At this level, what's absurd is how we think people should act towards their own benefit, when the women here are acting against their own benefit for the sake of a social structure that oppresses them in such a way as to force them to behave absurdly. When a person is conditioned to believe that this is how life is supposed to be, then they will work to keep the status quo in power, as well. As such, they are imprisoning themselves. With a society that can get women to self-police their own humility, putting themselves down at the hint of a compliment, it seems quite futile to advocate change, and yet the skit still makes a point, and in doing so advocates change.

On a much lighter note, in a skit called "Lunch at O'Nutter's," Schumer and her friends go to a Hooters-styled restaurant, but instead of women wearing tight, revealing uniforms, there are men wearing extremely revealing short-shorts. I submit that her intentions are to show the silliness of "breastaurants," such as Hooters. The theme and the outfits seem very silly, which seems to be exactly Schumer's point. However, the uniforms that we see at such real restaurants do not seem so silly, just because they actually exist. (They *are*, but we do not *think* of them as such.) Much like we see in the movie *Trainwreck*, there is an inversion of gender (and identity) roles. This inversion is an obvious absurdity, due to the fact that it would never happen. Yet, this "what if" scenario underscores the gender bias. In this episode, the server deftly flirts with the women, yet tries to establish a male comradery with the lone male. The women lob innuendo and jokes that seem awkward, but when the genders are reversed (and the environment is more "traditional"), it would seem perfectly reasonable. Much like the fantasies that we see played out on the screen, the lone, shy customer is lured out of his or her shell and becomes "sexier" because of it. Another absurdity would be the shy male, when we live in a society where men are rewarded for being less shy and women are expected to be shy. The awkwardness of the entire skit is the notion that the gender roles are so exceptionally reversed. The result is a hilarious sketch, one of Schumer's most memorable and funniest.

If there is an actual "battle" of the sexes, then it is a safe bet that the men are winning (and Schumer acknowledges this). The very fact that we can use war (or even competitive sports) as a metaphor to describe the relationship between the sexes can act as proof of this, since men are viewed to be quite competitive (stereotypically) in comparison to women. Much of Schumer's work (on TV or the big screen) seems to show this. With the fact that both men and women can (and do) enjoy sex, there is a major absurdity as to arguing this very point! Why argue about who is "winning" this battle? Isn't that, in itself, a rather futile and pointless act? Isn't it absurd?

Schumer the Sexistentialist

Why does Schumer pose a scathing analysis of male sexism? Does she do this because she wants to decry how the society operates, thereby promoting a change from a patriarchal society to something more open or inclusive? In *Trainwreck*, Schumer points out the hypocrisy that's inherent in sexism by reversing the gender roles. From a societal point of view, an important part of the absurdity of a movie like *Trainwreck* is to see a woman behaving and thinking in a stereotypically masculine way (which would seem quite absurd and comical because it is different). Amy Schumer's character ("Amy") is a serial philanderer who has learned to stay away from deep, meaningful relationships by watching her father (played by Colin Quinn). Schumer, who has a knack for self-deprecating humor (evident in all of her movies, stand up specials, book, and *Inside Amy Schumer*), manages to poke fun at the stereotypical male by allowing the audience to laugh at *her*. The qualities she embodies when she takes on the male role are laughable. In a way, she wants the audience to laugh at the stereotypical male that is part of our society.

At the same time, her focus is not on *the anonymous male.* The male characters are integral parts of Amy's life, and we can see how they affect Amy through various relational dynamics. The family dynamic that we see in the relationships in *Trainwreck* becomes quite complex as we see Schumer interact with her sister's family. She is quick to poke fun at her sister's husband (played by comedian Mike Birbiglia). However, when it comes to her nephew, even though she may poke fun at him (whether he is aware of it or not), she handles him with kid gloves. At the end of the movie, before she decides that she wants a relationship with her boyfriend, she talks to her nephew, who tells her that he planned to have Dr. Aaron Conners in his life. His opinion (the nephew's) spoke deeply to the commitment-phobe. Family is very important to Amy's character (in the movie). It was the motivating influence for why she became the person she did. It was also the influence for why she decided to change her ways.

In a subtle way, Schumer and Judd Apatow (the director) point out the absurdity inherent within the cycle of philandering that Schumer's character's father (Gordon Townsend) has set up for her with his early-life influence. Amy's character has seen this unhealthy lifestyle and decides (whether she is aware of it or not) to emulate this philosophy; when we flash back to how she was influenced by her father, her current existence seems inevitable. The concepts of sexism and gender disparity are not simple, even though her story seems to be. The sympathy that we (the audience members) have towards Schumer's character and her father lets us see that the serial philanderer isn't a villain.

This is a person who has a lonely heart. We can see it pretty obviously in one scene, when Amy walks out on her father. He calls out to her and, as the shot pans away from him, we (the audience) are left with a sense of loneliness. We see how Schumer has effectively pushed away most of the people who care about her. Even though this is a tired trope in the romantic comedy movie genre, Schumer pulls it off in a way that seems fresh. And, once again, we're left with a very great sense of loneliness. The serial philanderer seems to be a common phenomenon in our society. Coupling this with the notion that children will mimic their parents, it seems inevitable that this behavior will forever be of concern. Amy Schumer's stand-up act routinely exhibits (like many comics do) a cavalier attitude towards sex, and the philanderer seems to be the inevitable result of such thinking (to us, in our society).

Breaking the Rules

Schumer doesn't only poke fun at the masculine mystique by making her character a philanderer, she also places herself in the world of sports. Schumer portrays a writer who is absolutely clueless on all things sports and athletics. Schumer mispronounces team names, doesn't know who major athletes are, and herself maintains a total lack of athleticism. (The scene on the treadmill is one of my favorite examples of this.) She places herself in a world that she knows very little about to help showcase the fish out of water idea. Of course, this ineptitude may show what Schumer really sees when she observes athletes or major sports fanatics. By fictionalizing the situation, she points to something real—the existentialist turn.

Apatow and Schumer follow the traditional formula for a romantic comedy, but in order to do so within the fictional world Schumer has written for us, they have to break some very significant rules of the same formula. They create an adult comedy that does something that hasn't been done as well before. Amy Schumer's character in the film makes her own decisions and has a will that guides her into being promiscuous. She has free will to be the person that she is. Even though the audience sees her as shallow and self-involved, we laugh at the stumbles that she takes and sympathize with the character. We want her to make the right decisions. We know that the attractive doctor is right for her, but she has to make that decision for herself. We become like her sister: we know she is a good person who just needs to recognize the right man, Dr. Aaron Conners of course. Amy's character must assume responsibility for her actions, and we know we can't make those decisions for her—she's her own person.

She alienates all the people in her life that she cares about. Her poor decisions bring her to rock bottom. Then, and only then, she decides to make a change in her character to bring her family and loved ones back to her. *Trainwreck* seems to be an existentialist comedy. At the core of the story is one woman's quest to find meaning in hollow relationships. While meaninglessness saw her through much of her adult existence, that itself provided a meaning to her early life. When she meets a man who manages to unwittingly challenge her concept of relationships, she does not see any meaning in hollow one-night stands at all; she no longer sees meaning in meaninglessness. Thus, she makes changes in her life that reflect her new understanding of the meaning of a *relationship*, a positive meaning, rather than the negative meaning she's been using so far. As such, Amy gets her happily ever after ending, and the audience gets closure. This is quite typical of a romantic comedy.

So Judd Apatow and Amy Schumer create an atypical romantic comedy; however, they still manage to stay within the traditional confines and rules of what makes a contemporary romantic comedy. (This seems to resonate with the audience, since it did quite well at the box office.) That does not necessarily mean that the audiences received the message and agree with what she has to say; the audience too has the option to dismiss the movie as meaningless. *She's set it up that way for us*. We might think that there is no message, that Amy Schumer just wanted to tell a funny story, and the movie won't contradict that for us.

Trainwreck is an apt extension of Amy Schumer's voice in standup. Her work exemplifies an existentialist attitude towards sex and identity, a voice which she might just sneak into the public consciousness—because she also gives us something to laugh at, and a means of escaping meaning.

Rally the Troops

Absurdist humor tends to be understood as humor that is totally and utterly devoid of logic. Many people take this as something meaningless or non-sensical—slapstick, for instance. However, absurdity in Amy Schumer's work is something a bit darker than that, an existential absurdism. The notion of absurdity here deals with the idea that finding meaning is often a futile endeavor.

According to Camus, this meaninglessness is focused on man's constant search for a meaning of life. In Schumer's case, the meaninglessness is futility in the attempt to reconcile differences in gender and sexuality. What makes this an "absurdity" is the fact that in most of these cases, the problem is so systemic that the notion of attempting to evoke change puts us on an uphill journey not unlike that of Sisyphus, whom we just imagine as joyfully engaging in an act of futility. An eternal optimist may argue that Schumer will change the way men and women see each other socially.

Schumer's jokes act as a battle cry to those who want to institute change in a patriarchal society. If we were to think of Schumer as using humor to "rally the troops" (as it were), to create social change and outrage, we can see (just as Camus did) the paradox of this entire situation. The absurdity we see is an absurdity in reality, and we laugh because of how terrible it all seems.

Amy Schumer isn't trying to understand the meaning of life, but her methods of trying to understand gender and relationships mirror those of the existentialist who is. Much of her work contemplates the decisions that we make when we get into relationships, as well as how gender is defined in relation to a society.

The gender disparity that often is impressed upon us eventually becomes an environment that we condone; we internalize stereotypes and enact them whenever a woman takes a compliment. These social issues have been apparent in our society for a long time. Is it futile to think that her message could inspire a change in the culture? Perhaps so. Is *that* her point? Or is she just trying to get a few laughs? We should ask: is this a pointless exercise? Or is it *the point* to engage in a pointless exercise?

Whether all of this is actually getting to the point of Schumer's philosophies, or whether I am actually overanalyzing the material, the work of Amy Schumer does make important insights that serve to illustrate an existentialist perspective on gender relations. We know that our society is patriarchal, and that our patriarchal society is unjust, and yet all we can do is laugh about it.

9
Girls Just Wanna Have Mediated Fun

FERNANDO GABRIEL PAGNONI BERNS

Amy got a date! Finally!

In "Sex-Prep," Amy gets ready for sex. She goes to a hairdressing salon, shaves all the hair from her body, and even changes the shape of her anus. These are things every girl should do before sex, right? At least, that's what every form of media designed to be consumed by women would have us believe. But when the doorbell rings, she hides under her bed, waiting for her admirer to go away. The sketch ends with a message, stating that, "Amy never had sex again."

What goes wrong? Amy felt unattractive. All the magazines told her how to look, and since she does not look like Jessica Alba looks on magazine covers, it was better to put an end to the meeting before it really started. In "I'm So Bad," Amy further develops the connection between personal image, subjectivity, and market: "A lot of the women's magazines, they're supposed to, like, be confidence building, but they really just scare the shit out of you so you buy the products in them."

Amy is onto the idea that the main purpose of women's magazines is to control women's self-image by perpetuating beauty ideals. The constant demand to become "better," however, can have a negative effect on women's self-esteem, until women realize the impossibility of transforming themselves into two-dimensional embodiments of the media's version of perfection. Media not only engage with self-image, but also give advice on romantic relationships.

Virtually every women's magazine on the market has scores of articles on men, kink, and dating. Many people do not recognize the fact that their lives have become "mediatized," in the sense that they see themselves and their romantic lives in terms of what a magazine (the media market) tells them to buy, how to look, and how to act in order to perform well in life.

Many sketches on Schumer's show, *Inside Amy Schumer*, speak about "mediated" relationships—relationships conceived of within the context of ideals perpetuated by various media. People seem to engage with each other only in mediated terms, trying to fulfill expectations and images created and disseminated by media: Schumer's numerous parodies of TV shows and commercials demonstrate exactly this point.

In this sense, the series can be seen as a companion to Guy Debord's ideas about "the society of spectacle." Debord analyzes society as the sort of thing that is constructed through mediation and commodification. Debord predicted our distracted society would come to be populated with people paying attention only to the screens of cell phones and televisions. His philosophical thinking, however, is more complex than the idea of current society as saturated by images and zombified by television. When Debord describes the all-pervading commodification of society through spectacle, he does so in terms that identify spectacle as the social relationships between people filtered through the lens of media such as women's magazines.

Debord wrote one of the first texts of academic thinking on media and its weight in society—the intermingling of society, capitalism, and spectacle. *Inside Amy Schumer* offers an intelligent critique of social mediated relationships, completely in line with Guy Debord's philosophical thinking.

Debord Loves Amy (Because She Is Hot Enough)

Debord argues that modern society has undergone a significant development since mass industrialization. In modern production, people have moved away from merely striving to acquire the necessities of existence—food, shelter, and clothing—toward a life that aims at acquiring and maintaining a surplus (understood as the accumulation of money), thus changing the fundamental nature of the experience of living.

The society of the spectacle completely reconstructs reality and how we see things and each other: the society of the spectacle invites people to see every day through some kind of 3D glasses. The condition of being (existence with basic needs fulfilled) is replaced by the condition of having (commodities that make you feel in a better place than others). In turn, the condition of having is replaced by the *appearance* of having. After this last step, you're completely alienated from your own problems and social conditions. You think that you're better off than others, while you are actually not.

What exactly does Debord *mean* by "spectacle"? For Debord, spectacle is not a collection of images, but a social relation among people, *mediated by images*. For Schumer, relationships are mediated by the power of media, which indicate how she must look in order to be desirable. The message becomes a joke: if she does not meet these standards, prefabricated by media, then it is better for her to stay home.

An entire episode is dedicated to this idea. "Twelve Angry Men Inside Amy Schumer" (a parody of the play and movie *Twelve Angry Men*) revolves around Amy being judged by the twelve men of the title, who must decide if she is "hot enough" to be on television. At first, almost every man seems embarrassed to find Amy "hot enough" but slowly, they realize that beauty resides in the eye of the beholder. The problem here, however, is not whether Amy is hot or not. (For the record, the author maintains that such designations are completely subjective.) The real question is whether or not she answers the prefabricated measures of beauty that media impose upon women—a standard set according to the measure of the "reasonable chub." There are quite a few sketches about the ever-present consideration of Amy's hotness and how it is related to her position as a public figure. For example, in "Slow Your Roll," Amy must endure extreme diets sanctioned by famous people if she wants a third season of her show. In "You Would Bang Her?" a focus group on the show *Inside Amy Schumer* ends with everyone answering the title question. All of these sketches highlight the links between stardom, media, and self-image.

Debord observed that the spectacle actively alters human interactions and relationships. Amy plays this out to hilarious effect. In "Tyler Perry's Episode 208," Amy and her boyfriend, rather than talk to each other, fight over which movie to watch on TV. The fictional show "My Dream Breakup" (in "Down for Whatever") turns intimate relationships into spectacle, as the show revolves around people breaking-up on TV. The show stages and stylizes real breakups, which are broadcast to the pleasure of everyone watching. The breakup is real, but everything is so fake-looking that there is little difference between reality and fictional narrative.

Still, Amy's best satires are about reality shows. The fictional shows "How Will this Relationship End?" and "Love Tub" satirize the seemingly endless stream of TV shows that involve a commoditized romantic relationship as the main prize. Sometimes, there's cash money involved; and sometimes, the prize package includes romance *and* money (if the guy is a millionaire). Intimacy becomes spectacle, and winning love parallels winning money. Schumer deals directly with the issue of women's magazines in "Sex Tips." *Glamo*'s editor explicitly rejects any ideas for sex tips that her underlings present in earnest, instead encouraging the bizarre and extreme or, I argue, the spectacular.

Buying Is Better than Living

Images disseminated by media influence our daily lives; advertising prefabricates new desires and aspirations. Advertising now exerts actual influence like never before, due to the fact of the total intrusion of the consumer society within the fabric of our lives. Instead of merely trying to imitate life, advertising *becomes life*: families on TV seem happy because they have acquired product X, and real families try to emulate the emulation by acquiring the same products.

Among the best sketches of *Inside Amy Schumer* are those parodying TV advertising. When Amy speaks about the many qualities of a mattress ("Comforsleep") that make her forget that she was sexually molested, the joke is not on people who suffered sexual assaults, rammed their cars into orphanages, or were denied reasonable insurance claims. She's joking about the fact that advertising promises replacing your whole life with a better one: "Don't you deserve the kind of dark, dreamless sleep, where not even God can find you?" Rather than face your problems and resolve them, media invite you to forget them, thanks to a special mattress which helps people sleep no matter what is keeping them up at night. Advertising invites alienation. The real joke is on media that trivialize real tragedy by turning it into spectacle for massive consumption.

Advertising interprets and reduces the world for us with the use of simple narratives. In "Girl You Don't Need Makeup," Amy is visited by a pop group channeling The Backstreet Boys or 'N Sync. Their song invites Amy to look more natural, so she wipes the excessive make-up from her face. The result, however, is far from the contemporary societal concept of ideal female beauty, so the boy band pushes Amy to apply some *more* make-up on her face (lots and lots of makeup).

The sketch is a great illustration of Debord's thinking: not only is the message ambivalent—look natural, but laboriously natural! Look girlier!—but the messengers are the embodiment of prefabricated media. Boy bands are manufactured by large corporations. They determine what your next idol will resemble before their music ever hits the streets. Audiences do not actually choose: these people are your lovely idols and you will scream for them! Because somebody—not you—has decided that you should.

In *Comments on the Society of Spectacle*, Debord examines the phenomenon of celebrity culture. Debord observes that fame has acquired more importance than the value of anything one might actually be capable of doing. As embodiments of the spectacle, celebrities renounce all autonomous qualities in order to identify themselves with the status quo. After all, celebrities are commodities themselves. Schumer illustrates this aspect of Debord's theory brilliantly.

One recurrent sketch in the show is Amy acting like a selfish celebrity who is focused exclusively on how she is represented to members of her ever-adoring public. In "Publicity Stunt," Amy regrets her negative media image, so she decides to "pity fuck a prom loser" as a way to show some tenderness to the audience. After finding the perfect date on YouTube, she comes to the prom and (of course) everything goes wrong, as her date actually has a real date and, worse, the boy does not even know who Amy Schumer is. A fight ensues. Later, in the office, she evaluates the whole misadventure. Nonetheless, she is happy: in the photos of prom night, her arms look thin. This manipulative, narcissistic version of Amy embraces the trend of thin bodies rather than fight the prejudice using the power that she has as a woman working in media. Her character is completely alienated from the entire experience, focused solely on a superficial detail about how her arms look in a representation of the experience.

I contrast "Publicity Stunt" with another self-aware sketch "I'm Sorry," in which a group of women innovators, all of whom are leading authorities in their fields, are invited to a panel for "Women Innovating: Females in Innovation Conference 2015". During the panel, they focus more on apologizing for each little thing going wrong—like interrupting each other—than they do talking about their research. As women innovators, they are removed from the spectacle and thus, they feel uneasy, even if they are doing much more for humanity than any movie diva. The unity between these sketches is how Schumer illustrates Debord's thinking: spectacle—movie personalities, for example—occupies much more space in media than do serious issues.

Mecha-Amy

Debord's ideas can be applied to people's current reliance on technology. Today, Debord would almost certainly extend his analysis of the spectacle to the internet and social media, since Facebook, Instagram, Twitter and Snapchat commodify our friendships, thoughts, and emotions ("I'm blue! Look at the sad face of my emoticon!") for everyone to see, including strangers.

What do you do when you think that you have found the perfect mate? Stalk him through a careful surveillance of his social media profiles, of course! His accounts will tell you everything you want to know about him. In "Search History," Amy reviews her boyfriend's browsing history, only to find such websites as "Only attracted to girlfriend" and "How to explain to your girlfriend that you're extremely wealthy." Amy has done the same thing before. In "One Night Stand," she decides that the man she has just met the night before is the love of her life. To great comedic effect, she's wrong. After all, the episode is called "Bad Decisions." Amy was just a one-night stand without further consequence.

Modern technology is incredibly useful, but it also *engineers* our behavior. It reduces our lives to a daily series of commodity exchanges. In "Sext Photographer," Amy cannot refuse a request from a crush, who asks for erotic pics and messages from her. But her anxiety about her body as commodity hilariously increases as she pushes herself to extremes—including hiring an expert in sexy photography to ensure the spectacle is properly portrayed, and anything real is camouflaged. Through a "spectacularized" life, we assign the meaning of our existence to something that is initially external to our subjectivity, but which manages to enslave us to the circulation of representations. Just think about poor Amy trying to present herself as "sexy" ("sexiness" as media understand the term). Rather than being a moment for spontaneous, natural fun, the flirting becomes a horrid descent into stress. The spectacle invites people to see things they way they are represented, and then it traps them in this hell of mass produced images, deliberately obscuring the reality of what is being represented.

The rise of media and spectacle are vehicles for separation from friends, community and even our sense of self.

Rather than engage in real, face-to-face communication, we prefer to fix our gaze on a screen and ignore the people sitting next to us. This sustains the creation of the "lonely crowd," and it originates from the loss of communication between people. *The Society of the Spectacle*'s first chapter is entitled "Separation Perfected," a feature that Debord describes as the "alpha and omega of the spectacle."

Let me get back to "Sext Photographer." When Amy receives the message from "Bobby," she panics and calls a friend (Jess) for advice. Jess only furthers Amy's sense of anxiety, balking at the idea that Amy is taking the pictures herself. The only thing that she does know is that people expect her to be able to produce a prefabricated intimacy: wet hair, sexy faces, close shots of her genitalia, and so forth. She doesn't consider the possibility of real intimacy, instead defaulting to the expression of a stylized, sanitized surface. Rather than showing herself as she is, Amy chooses spectacle. Soon enough, the sext photographer arrives, with instructions like, "Don't forget your duck mouth," "Smile like you don't have Spanx on!" and "There's a spider in your hair!" Spectacle wins over reality.

Spectacle presents itself as superior, *better*, than the world. With people trying to understand themselves through a representation, they lose all hope of a coherent life. As a consequence, people become alienated. As Debord argues, the more the spectators recognize themselves within spectacularized images, the less they understand their own existence and desires. At the core of spectacle, there is only isolation; direct human relations are replaced with the fragmented obedience to spectacle.

Debord did not necessarily believe that new technology was a bad thing *per se*. He objected in particular to the use of media for economic profit. The spectacle, which is driven solely by economic profit, replaces lived reality with the "contemplation of the spectacle." There's no separation between material real life and the false representation of the spectacle. They are intertwined to such a degree that any glimpse of truth is negated and reduced to mere appearance.

Oh My God, That Is So Sad

Another widely-discussed effect produced by spectacle is alienation. The alienation of the spectator is expressed like this: the more the spectator contemplates, the less they live.

Referring to the Marxist concept of false consciousness, Debord describes how the spectacle conceals the relations among people and classes of people. The spectacle works as opium for the masses, a device that reinforces the status quo and alienates people from their own condition as members of an exploited socio-economic class.

Inside Amy Schumer satirizes this lack of comprehension about the real state of subordination of people to media. "Allergic to Nuts" begins with a sketch called "Judging Strippers," focused on a group of upper-class women in a gym. They look slightly bored, standing by a window literally looking down at strippers leaving work in the morning. The women judge the strippers in the most condescending ways possible (assuming that they have bad relationships with their fathers and feeling bad for them, since the strippers have to give up their bodies to the gaze of men as a means of life). They act as if they were women living a completely different life. Their rude gym teacher comes in and starts to push them hard to start pole-dancing, yelling "Whores! Whores! You're all whores!" All the women comply, as they want keep their bodies thin so they can be attractive to men.

The sketch points to the absurd ways women are pushed to feel about their bodies and their sexuality. The upper-class women do not recognize the fact that they share many issues with the strippers, such as how they model their bodies to fit an eroticized spectacle. Like the strippers, these women are exploited by media, but they are too alienated to understand their own situation. The sketch invites women to realize their own role within society and to regain control over their own bodies. Also, it leads to a reflection on the overly simplistic idea that a stripper (or sex worker) has fallen into that job because of "bad relations" with her father, which is really a reduction to the absurd. The sketch reveals that the reasons that lead a woman to alienate herself from her body are not just personal, but instead guided by political and social structures. Thus, the sketch invites to fight against these rigid structures that relegate women to a subordinate role.

This Murder Is Sponsored By . . .

The society of the spectacle presents, through a disjointed synthesis of images and politics, a form of "real" world—an integrated spectacle that leaves viewers distracted from the real conditions of social life. This disjointed nature is overlooked, thanks to the great value that we attribute to visibility. If something is being broadcast, we assume that it must be real, in the sense that it must be important to us. The spectacle has led us to think this way, and we naturally disregard the resulting internal contradiction.

Debord observes that spectacle creates coherence as opposed to communication, unity from disjunction. For instance, TV news depicting a dramatic event might be preceded by a glamorous advertisement, blending real life, pain, commodities and aesthetics into one unified spectacle. TV newscasts use music to emphasize real dramatic situations, recasting them in the light of a fictional narrative.

Amy Schumer illustrates this infelicitous blending of politics and show in "Gang Bang." Amy hosts her own gang bang as a feminist statement, and she thanks her sponsor "the good people at Sea Spray for providing all the cranberry juice I'll be drinking throughout the day." When the men who had accepted the invitation turn out to be ugly, she cancels the gang bang. But when the participants don't seem to be disappointed enough, she starts comparing herself to other women (negatively, of course) and reinstates the gang bang. There's a flagrant contradiction between her supposedly feminist goals and the pathological relation she has with her own self-image—and that's the joke.

Finally, Some Verité

Debord claims that it is only through moving away from the spectacular that people can gain a real sense of meaning. But is this possible? Can moments of truth be found within our mediated world?

It is not by chance that Amy leaves the real meaning for the end. Each episode ends with an "Amy Goes Deep" segment in which, precisely, she goes beneath the surface of the spectacle. These segments are interviews about sex, business, and gender. The segment is funny, but it's also a moment where there is almost no spectacle. The emphasis on "verité" interviews works to anchor the show in something "real," within a world of sketches and mediated relationships. Almost all of the people interviewed work in some type of "mediatized" work: they are sexual performers, porn actresses, and gigolos. These are all people who depend on their image and how it, in turn, responds to the dictates of the consumer society. Almost all of the interviewees are people who have been turned into commodities. It's precisely for this reason that Amy leaves the interviews for the end, to show how the human side escapes from the society of the spectacle—what's left in the margins of the media.

Following this idea, sometimes the show ends with some bloopers, a brief glimpse of the reality behind the fiction. This closure is the ultimate subversive act: it displays how the "spectacle" is made, how fictitious it is. These rough drafts explicitly display what has gone wrong, thus breaking any identification with the scene and the characters. The bloopers show, in short, what should be discarded: that what we see is pure fiction, not reality. And we should not mistake one with the other.

III

Misbehaving

10
Multiple Murderer Emily Middleton

CHARLENE ELSBY

Amy Schumer stars in the movie *Snatched*, along with Goldie Hawn, who, if the Internet is to be believed, Amy dragged out of retirement because she wanted Goldie Hawn to be her mother. The film was written by Katie Dippold, obviously a comic master, and tweaked throughout filming to suit the characters. (Schumer says in an interview with *Hollywood Reporter* that some of the things Hawn says in the film are things her mother has actually said.)

This collaboration of great minds results in the sophisticated study of human behavior, natural causality, and moral culpability that is *Snatched*. The movie focuses on the two women, kidnapped in Ecuador, and demands that we follow, along with their adventures, an increasingly nuanced theory of personal responsibility, presented through several hypothetical case studies. Throughout the film, Amy pretends to be Emily, a thirty-something woman whose purchase of a non-refundable vacation acts as a catalyst for the ensuing shenanigans. (Nice try, Amy, we can tell it's you.) Her mother, cat-woman Linda Middleton, acts against her own better judgment and accompanies her daughter on the ill-fated trip.

Although Emily and Linda make very different choices in life, consider different reasons for making those choices, and evidence different values in constructing reasons to make those choices, they both end up in the same place—kidnapped in Ecuador. This fatalist view of the universe informs most of the movie. Watching the film, we always know that, all else being equal, they were always fated to be kidnapped in Ecuador, and we also know that everything will work out in the end.

Between the beginning and the end, the capacity for human freedom remains, and Emily and Linda set us the task of recognizing what exactly we contribute to the consequences of our actions, and what (on the other hand) the universe contributes to those same actions. As the movie begins, a thesis statement pops up on the screen: "In the Spring of 2017, two American women were abducted fifty kilometers outside Puerto Cayo, Ecuador. What followed was a tale of violence, mayhem, and a reckless disregard for human life. The kidnappers did bad stuff, too."

We immediately forget this warning as soon as it's gone, though, choosing to believe that Emily and her mother are "the good guys" and the Ecuadorian kidnappers are "the bad guys." This informs our interpretation of the moral worth of their actions, so that we think it's natural to allow Emily to return to the United States as a multiple murderer and carry on, going on more vacations with her complicit mother, while an Ecuadorian man forced by his environment to live a criminal lifestyle is left behind to mourn the loss of his nephew and brother. But let's not get too far ahead of ourselves. We'll start back at the start.

Help Me Put the Fun in Non-Refundable

This is the phrase Emily uses to manipulate her Mom into disregarding all of her legitimate concerns for her own safety and that of her daughter's, in order to finish a line of causality that started at some point in the past when Emily decided she could predict the future far enough not to require refundable tickets. We find this completely believable, as so far Emily has lost her job due to inattention, been dumped by her boyfriend (who was no prize peach, thus indicating some earlier deficiency in Emily's judgment) and failed to find a replacement friend on *the Internet*, which is huge.

Although Linda Middleton is clearly a cautious woman and concerned for her daughter's safety, that cautious sort of lifestyle has kept her no safer from her daughter's mistakes. She still ends up in Ecuador, where she slathers on the sunscreen, in a valiant effort to squelch the effects of *the sun* itself, which is no minor task. In short, Linda Middleton is a hero whose fight extends beyond the whims of her daughter to include forces of nature, against which she believes she has a fighting chance. And she would be right, if it weren't for that daughter of hers.

Linda warns Emily that perhaps she shouldn't go out drinking in a foreign country with strange men. She attempts to use reverse psychology on Emily, saying, "Well, drinking with a man in a foreign country . . . You know? It's a smart, responsible thing to do." But Emily is immune to her mother's psychological tricks, and replies, "Thank you. I know that that is sincere, and I thank you." This is our first case study of personal responsibility.

So far, Emily has dragged her mother to a foreign country, met an odd woman (Ruth) who foreshadows her kidnapping, and decides to go out drinking anyway. You might want to say that Emily has right set herself up for a kidnapping and ignored all the warning signs leading up to it, and that Emily is therefore to blame. But in the tally of bad stuff, that wouldn't be right.

Kidnapping Emily and Linda is not one of the bad things Emily has done. The kidnappers did that (remember, the kidnappers did bad stuff too). Just because Emily was drinking, just because she was hanging around with strangers and sometimes kicking them in the face, just because she's tits out, does not mean that she kidnapped herself. That doesn't even make sense, and you should be ashamed for thinking it.

The difference here is with regard to the *origin of actions*, a question of who literally *did the thing* we're trying to blame them for. Who was it who actually *moved their limbs* in such a way that a bad thing happened? We ascribe responsibility to people based on whether they originate the action for which they are meant to be responsible. Emily bought non-refundable tickets and is therefore responsible for buying non-refundable tickets. Emily went out drinking and is therefore responsible for crawling into bed drunk. The kidnappers kidnapped her, and they are responsible for kidnapping her.

This way of thinking avoids blaming someone for *the entire chain of causality* resulting from their actions. Just because Emily bought a non-refundable ticket does not mean that she is now responsible for everything that everyone in Ecuador does. She is not responsible for her mother spitting out her welcome beverage, and she is not responsible for whatever that attractive lady at the bar does after Emily tells her to go away because she's a distraction. If we held everyone responsible for *everything* that came about as a result of their actions, everyone would be fucked.

There's got to be some point at which we *cut off* the chain of personal responsibility, and we're just going to have to do that on a case-by-case basis. For instance, while Morgado wasn't the one actually in the truck kidnapping Emily and Linda, he was the guy giving the orders to the guys who did, so he could be held responsible. But we can't blame Emily. Maybe it was Linda—if she wasn't so busy reading her book that night, maybe she could have gotten Emily to bed a bit sooner, before she agreed to go on a driving tour of Ecuador. We know that doesn't make sense, though, and it also doesn't make sense to blame Emily for something that *someone else did*.

I Saw His Brains

Let's talk about the brutal murder of Hector Morgado's nephew. Linda and Emily have been kidnapped at this point, dragged into a van by masked jerks who plan to ransom them. Linda wanted to take the freeway back to the resort, but Emily's superior wisdom led them along the path of putative waterfalls and rainbows. Meanwhile, Linda is also the only one to notice the men in the van beside them putting on masks. She makes one last-ditch effort to save them all, but nobody listens. Emily wakes up in some hole with her mother. Linda is reading a magazine that she chooses to believe is about some local farming practices. (Linda is able to bend space-time like that.) Morgado reveals his plot to ransom them, and Emily reveals her super secret PIN. Soon, they have to be moved and are shoved in the trunk of a car.

Because Linda watches *Dateline*, she knows that she can escape the trunk by pulling on some cord. It seems like a good feature to have in car trunks, just in case anyone ever gets stuck in there. So they jump out of the back of this car and hitch a ride on a passing truck. An Ecuadorian man chases them, but Emily and Linda reach the truck before he does and get on the back. Emily finds a shovel and thwacks their pursuer. For an off-screen while, they are apparently silent, but when the truck stops and tells them to get off, Emily wants to confirm her kill: "Ma, do you think there's any way that, like, maybe that guy's okay?" Linda responds, "I saw his brains."

Is Emily *responsible* for his death? According to a theory based on the origin of action, yes she is. She was the one who picked up the shovel and thwacked him with it, hard enough for his brains to come out. Can we come up with alternative theories of personal responsibility to let Emily off the hook? Of course we can, and as a moral monster, she's counting on us to do it. So we find someone else to blame, someone whose actions directly contributed to the murder. Perhaps we can blame the kidnapper himself. After all, if he hadn't been chasing the truck in the first place, he wouldn't have been within shovel's reach for Emily to thwack him. But we're also sure he was under orders from Morgado. If he didn't make a solid effort to get those women back (and the money he thinks they're worth), then he would have displeased Morgado, and would perhaps be in even more trouble. Maybe we assume that he made some kind of rational calculation and determined that he would rather have his brains thwacked out by Emily's shovel than to return to Morgado empty-handed. We can speculate all we want, but there's still a sense in which Emily is definitely responsible. She had the shovel.

When Emily and Morgado meet again, she apologizes for killing his nephew—or does she? She gives him one of those non-apologies where she explicitly says she's sorry, but the implication is definitely that it wasn't at all her fault. So there's this sense of being *sorry* that doesn't imply that the person who is sorry is responsible for whatever has gone wrong, and that's the one Emily uses in her so-called apology. She says: "I'm sorry. But listen, you kidnapped us. And that's what motivated that. So, like that is on you."

The implied version of personal responsibility in our second case study diverges from the first. In addition to who originated the action, we now have to account for who is responsible for creating the situation in which that action was possible. After all, if Hector Morgado hadn't recruited his nephew into a life of kidnapping tourists, he wouldn't have been in the situation to get hit with a shovel. Even though Emily actually hit him with a shovel, she in no way contributed to the situation she was in. She was literally taken by force and locked in the trunk of a car with her arms tied.

We interpret the murder of Morgado's nephew as part of her ascent to freedom. First, you untie the knots, then you jump out of the trunk, then you find a passing truck to make your escape, then you disable the pursuing kidnapper with a nearby shovel. Although she wasn't *physically forced* to thwack him, her immediate other option was to be re-confined in a car trunk, and she has a phobia about that. Her options were limited, and they were limited by Morgado.

Still, we think that she did have options. And her explanation is weak. We like to think that once you're kidnapped in Ecuador, you can do whatever you like, and just get away with it like nothing happened. We sweep personal responsibility under the rug and claim that, okay, well, Hector Morgado *motivated* that killing, and therefore it's really his fault. But he didn't kill his nephew. Emily *meant* to hit him with a shovel, and she did, and then he died.

Now wait a second, does that mean that we can go back to Emily's kidnapping and somehow blame her for that, too? Because she caused a situation in which she could be kidnapped? *No!* In no way did she *threaten, persuade, or coerce* her kidnappers into kidnapping her. Get your head on straight and stop victim blaming. There's no such thing as posting too many Instagram photos and thereby forcing someone to kidnap you.

So we can sometimes but not always refer to the *motivation* for an action in order to excuse ourselves from its consequences, because not too many motivations justify murder. In response to Emily's blame shift, Morgado claims that due to some law of the universe, "You took someone from my family. I must take someone from yours." This similarly sketchy justification *motivates* him to try to kill Linda, but we don't think that it's *justified*, and so we're happy enough when Emily commits her second heinous murder.

And That Was Before You Murdered His Son

"Accidentally murdered," Emily says in response to Linda's fear of Morgado's retribution for yet another family member killed by American tourist and multiple murderer Emily Middleton.

What was she thinking, picking up that spear gun? She was thinking that she could threaten Morgado's men with the spear gun, cause a distraction, and that she and her mother would then somehow get away. But the spear gun goes off and shoots Hector Morgado's only son. Emily's second murder causes the necessary distraction, and Linda and Emily escape.

Is Emily a bloodthirsty killer *now*? I mean, she meant to pick up the spear gun, and she meant to use it to threaten the Morgados. According to the logic above, that according to which she justified killing the nephew, the Morgados would then be justified in just taking out the Middletons. But instead, they lose a man, while the Middletons run off, having committed another murder. In response to Emily's moral crisis after the second murder, her callous mother assures her, "You are a very gifted murderer."

This case study reminds us that, when we judge someone's relative blameworthiness or innocence, we tend to not only take into account who originated the action (in this case, Emily) along with any mitigating situations (in this case, the continued threat of confinement and physical harm), we also take into account someone's *intention*. Emily picked up the spear gun with *an* intent—to threaten people, but not with the intent to *shoot* it. She didn't intend to kill anyone, although she did intend to threaten them. In our calculations, this seems to make her less blameworthy.

When we talk just about facts about what happened, the story depends on how you tell it. We might say that Morgado's only son was shot while he was attempting recapture some kidnapped American tourists, and then he seems to be the blameworthy one. Or we could say that Emily Middleton picked up a spear gun with the intent to threaten someone and then killed them, and then she seems to be the blameworthy one. Depending on perspective, Emily is a multiple murderer or a victim of circumstance. But when we take into account *intent*—the fact that she didn't intend to kill anyone—we think her as not blameworthy for the fact that it happened.

Of course, the man wouldn't have died if she *hadn't* picked up the spear gun, and it's not clear whether it went off on its own or if she accidentally fired it, but all in all, it seems a chance occurrence. And when we say that something happened by "chance," all we mean is that nobody intended for it to happen. What happened is that Emily didn't know that the spear gun would go off when she picked it up. It happens.

On the whole, I think that we tend to judge Emily's murders from an Aristotelian standpoint. It just so happens that in Aristotle's *Nicomachean Ethics*, he mentions a whole bunch of similar scenarios where people accidentally kill or maim other people—situations in which, Aristotle believes, they are innocent by virtue of their ignorance:

> A man may be ignorant, then, of who he is, what he is doing, what or whom he is acting on, and sometimes also what (for instance, what instrument) he is doing it with, and to what end (for instance, for safety), and how he is doing it (for instance, whether gently or violently). Now no one could be ignorant of all of these unless he were mad, and evidently also he could not be ignorant of the agent; for how could he not know himself? But of what he is doing a man might be ignorant, as for instance people say 'it slipped out of their mouths as they were speaking', or 'they did not know it was a secret', as Aeschylus said of the mysteries, or a man might say he 'let it go off when he merely wanted to show its working', as the man did with the catapult. Again, one might think one's son was an enemy, as Merope did, or that a pointed spear had a button on it, or that a stone was pumice-stone; or one might give a man a draught to save him, and really kill him; or one might want to touch a man, as people do in sparring, and really strike him. The ignorance may relate, then, to any of these things—of the circumstances of the action—and the man who was ignorant of any of these is thought to have acted involuntarily, and especially if he was ignorant on the most important points; and these are thought to be what he is doing and with what aim. Further, the doing of an act that is called involuntary in virtue of ignorance of this sort must be painful and involve regret. (Aristotle, *Nicomachean Ethics* III.2, 1111a3–1111a21)

If the analogy holds between Aristotle's account of accidents based on ignorance and Emily's situation, she is innocent of both murders. Like the man who, in sparring, means only to touch someone and accidentally strikes them, Emily meant to get Morgado's nephew off the back of her getaway truck and kills him. And like the man who meant to show his catapult was working, or the one who thought his spear was dulled, so was Emily's spear gun murder a result of her ignorance of how spear guns work. If there were any doubt as to her guilt, we can reassure ourselves by pointing to the fact that *she felt badly* about killing those people, after the fact, thus demonstrating that she didn't really mean to do it.

In other words, if Emily knew that Morgado's nephew would die when she hit him with the shovel, she probably wouldn't have done it. And if she knew that Morgado's son would die when she picked up the spear gun, she probably wouldn't have done it. Therefore, by virtue of her own ignorance, we can excuse her multiple murders in the court of public opinion and enjoy the movie.

11
The Unruly Woman

CECILIA LI

Amy Schumer has risen to fame within a widespread explosion of female comedy.

When we talk about Amy Schumer, some other key players also come to mind: Lena Dunham of HBO's *Girls*; Comedy Central's Ilana Glazer and Abbi Jacobson of *Broad City*; and Mindy Kaling of *The Mindy Project*.

The message is clear. These unruly women openly express their shameful habits, embrace their romantic incongruities, and bring to life some of the less pleasant but nonetheless real aspects of a woman's experience. Their works explore the enduring conflicts in the relationships between a woman and her appearance, sexuality, men, other women, her independence and sense of self—all the while baring some of the more awkward and cringe-worthy moments of growing up in the era of post-feminism and glossy billboard ads of beautiful models.

Female comedy is by no means a new thing. There have been, of course, early pioneers like Joan Rivers, Phyllis Diller, and more recently Sarah Silverman. But the surprising vulnerability and the eerie honesty with which the new generation brings forth their experiences are both refreshing and touching. Amy Schumer, the thirty-something, blonde, Long Island native is at the front and center of what I call *the phenomenon of the unruly woman*. Beyond the usual dirty jokes about body parts, her comedy explores themes of self-acceptance and an unwavering search for authenticity, one mistake at a time.

Schumer's popularity is matched by few. With her newfound fame comes closer scrutiny and backlash. Emily Nussbaum, in a review of the third season of *Inside Amy Schumer* writes, "It's happened again and again to the new wave of female TV creators, the Tinas and Mindys and Lenas, whose fans want role models as well as artists—a demand that many female comics embrace but that's rarely required of men. Louis C.K., whose show is having a terrific rebound season, doesn't owe his fans anything except comedy" (*The New Yorker,* May 11th 2015).[1]

The idea that artistic expression ought to serve as some kind of moral guidance to our lives seems archaic. After all, TV has given us Tony Soprano, Walter White, and Dexter Morgan. But Amy Schumer and her trailblazing peers prove that the public not only expect them to confirm that women can be funny. They're also expected not just to be feminists, but even the *right kind* of feminists. Do they stand up for the right issues? Are their works accurately reflecting all aspects of the female experience? Do they have the *right* political and social stances? *Do we have a right to expect all of this from them?*

Plato and the Poets

Plato was famously unfriendly to "poetry," which in his time meant all kinds of storytelling. Throughout his life, he devoted several important works to describing the "ancient quarrel" between philosophy and poetry (which he talks about in the *Republic*).

Plato's case against poetry was both complex and puzzling. Plato was concerned with the content of poetry, its

---

[1] EDITORS' NOTE: It seems that in 2018, we do expect more from Louis C.K. than comedy. We also expect him not to show his penis to people who don't want to see it, but we're willing to let him get away with it, because *he's a complex individual worthy of our consideration*. The fact that public opinion is siding in favor of giving this exhibitionist masturbator a second chance proves the point Li is making.

powerful influence over the development of young people, and its ability to get us to do away with our rational capacities by appealing to our baser desires. We can imagine how Plato might have responded to Amy Schumer, in her attempt to broaden the scope of female representation by highlighting some of the messier and unpleasant aspects of female identity. The central thesis of Plato's criticism against poetry is still pertinent to the ways in which we think about our relationship to the media and the influence media exercise over us.

Plato's discussion of the value of poetry occurs within the context of a larger discussion about how a city and a state should embody justice. The central character in Plato's dialogue and his real-life mentor, Socrates, describes the ideal city—that which most embodies justice. Along the way, he outlines an educational program for the Guardian class—an important group of selected individuals serving in the military class, whose training will prepare them for future roles as Philosopher Kings. The Guardians will undergo a strict regimen of physical training, in addition to education in music and poetry. The former is meant to strengthen the body, while the latter aims to develop the correct character traits in the souls of the young.

Plato recognized the powerful influence of poets as storytellers, especially on young people. Socrates asks, "You know, don't you, that the beginning of any process is most important, especially for anything young and tender? It's at that time that it's most malleable and takes on any pattern one wishes to impress on it" (*Republic,* 377a10–b1). Because children and young adults have yet to develop a fixed character, their souls are more open to persuasion and influence. Therefore, Plato argued, it is of the utmost importance to supervise the storytellers and the kind of stories that can be admitted into the ideal city: "We'll select their stories whenever they are fine or beautiful and reject them when they aren't" (*Republic*, 377b8–10). To select stories that are "fine" and "beautiful," Plato gives an extensive list of rules of storytelling that range anywhere from the depiction of gods to the afterlife.

Amy Schumer, a storyteller in her own right, is someone Plato might have wanted to supervise. Although Schumer's work is not directly part of any formal education, her presence and success in our culture speaks to the impact that her insights and worldview have on us. Given that the majority of Schumer's demographic is made up of young women, she walks a fine line between artistic creativity and role model. This vaguely defined collection of individuals we call "society" expects her to represent and to shape the female interest, as well as be funny.

One of Plato's rules for storytellers is that they ought not to depict their heroes as succumbing to excessive emotions and bearing misfortunes publicly. He tells us that the heroes in these stories ought to "least give way to lamentations and bear misfortune most quietly when it strikes" (*Republic,* 387e4–5). In other words, when Plato considers what kind of stories our young people should be exposed to, he excludes anything with a whiny protagonist who bears any misfortune with anything less than supreme fortitude. Plato explains his reasons for this:

> If our young people . . . listen to these stories without ridiculing them as not worth hearing, it's hardly likely that they'll consider the things described in them to be unworthy of mere human beings like themselves or that they'll rebuke themselves for doing or saying similar things when misfortune strikes. Instead, they'll feel neither shame nor restraint but groan and lament at even insignificant misfortunes. (*Republic,* 388d1–6)

Plato believed that the heroes or heroines of our stories ought to serve as models of moral virtue. We should not depict them as dwelling on their feelings, publicly suffering, or embracing their faults. This, in Plato's eyes, allows the spectators to feel neither shame nor restraint about their own shortcomings.

Amy Schumer, Corrupter of Souls

Amy Schumer, ever the heroine of her own life story, has adopted the opposite mantra to Plato. In her book, *The Girl with the Lower Back Tattoo*, Schumer argues for self-acceptance by publicly acknowledging her own blunders. She does so because she says it makes her more human. She does so because mistakes are a part of life. And most of all, she does so because by acknowledging your own shortcomings, you can mitigate some of those feelings of shame that come along with being human. In her closing chapter, Amy describes the consequence of a permanent mistake she made when she was nineteen (the dreaded lower back tattoo):

> So now, fifteen years later, I'm thirty-five, and any time I'm in a bathing suit people immediately know in their hearts that I'm trash. Any time I take my clothes off for the first time in front of a man and he sees it, he also knows in his heart that I'm trash and that I make poor, poor decisions. And now that the paparazzi think it's interesting to take photos of me doing absolutely nothing noteworthy on a beach somewhere, the whole world has been treated to photos of my lower back tattoo hovering crookedly over my bikini bottoms. But I promise you from the bottom of my heart I don't care. I wear my mistakes like badges of honor, and I celebrate them. They make me human. Now that all of my work, my relationships, my tweets, my body parts, and my sandwiches are publicly analyzed, I'm proud that I labeled myself a flawed, normal human before anyone else did. I beat all the critics and Internet trolls to the punch. I've been called everything in the book, but I already branded myself a tramp, so the haters are going to have to come up with something fresh. (pp. 310–11)

Schumer's complete acceptance of human flaws means that, unfortunately, *The Girl with the Lower Back Tattoo* won't be admitted into Plato's ideal city. For Plato, mistakes should not be worn like badges of honor, and they definitely should not be celebrated. The goal of life is not to accept our mere humanly self, but rather to strive for a virtuously divine life by emulating those who exemplify moral ideals. Amy, on the other hand, wants to expand our palette for female representation in popular culture. She writes on the significance of her tattoo today: "It reminds me that it's important to let yourself be vulnerable, to lose control and make a mistake" (p. 314). She tells us that her vulnerability is her greatest strength. She's the unruly woman—neither a victim, nor an avenging superwoman. She is unpleasant and messy, smart and ditzy. To quote Amy quoting Walt Whitman, "I contain multitudes."

By the end of the *Republic*, Plato's critique of poetry and storytellers has come to depend on his own views on the nature of the world and human psychology. Among their many dangers, the most serious charge against poetry is that, "with a few exceptions, it is able to corrupt even decent people, for that's surely an altogether terrible thing" (*Republic,* 605c5–7). To understand why Plato thought that poetry has the power to corrupt even the most decent people, we have to look at his views on human psychology.

Plato famously thought that the soul was comprised of three parts: the appetitive, spirited and rational. The appetitive part of the soul is responsible for our desires for bodily pleasures of food, drink and sex. The spirited part is responsible for our desires associated with feelings of shame, anger and pity. And the rational part of the soul is concerned with calculation, in determining what is best.

Plato believed that the just person—one who lives a happy and virtuous life—is someone whose soul is in harmony. This means that each part of the soul must perform its own proper work, with the rational part regulating and controlling the spirited and appetitive parts. In this way, our appetitive and spirited desires are always kept in check by our rational judgment for what is best. Plato's most serious charge against poetry is that it can convince even the most self-controlled and just person to lower her guard against indulging in the lower parts of the soul.

Given the dramatic context of storytelling and poetry, we might think that it is harmless to take pleasure in viewing other people weeping, lamenting and indulging in their desires, but Plato worried that this actually leads to the lower parts of our soul growing so large that they begin to overtake our rational judgment.

Schumer has no such worry. In her ongoing penchant for human messiness, Schumer dedicates a chapter of her book to "Secret Bad Habits." She writes about her lifelong battle with junk food, overindulging, and body image. On her ravenous young self, Schumer writes,

> In college, my roommate Denise couldn't leave her food lying around because I'd come home from class or the bar and find a box of Twinkies and eat the whole thing. She'd make a tray of lasagna, and I'd slowly, square by square, eat the entire dish. I'd wake up like Garfield to her screaming my name. I had to tell her to start hiding it from me. I couldn't even know it was in the house. She started running out of places to hide her snacks because I would always find them. I would ransack my own apartment like the Gestapo. One night she brought a guy home, and he found a box of Devil Dogs under her pillow. He was really weirded out. She was totally embarrassed and blamed me, but I of course acted like I didn't know what she was talking about. (p. 215)

To put it in Platonic terms, the parts of young Amy's soul are in conflict with each other. On the one hand, the rational part of her soul tells her roommate to hide food from her. Amy knows that this is best thing to do, because excessive eating is not only bad for her, but that she is also being a pretty crappy roommate. On the other hand, Amy is ruled by her appetitive desires. According to Plato's theory, young Amy lacks self-control to do what is best, because her appetitive soul has grown so large that it rules and dominates her capacity for rational judgment.

Not only is young Amy an unjust person in Plato's eyes, she is causing harm as a storyteller. Amy tells us about her insatiable appetites with humor and candor. We laugh and might even sympathize with her a little. After all, who hasn't ordered pastitzza at three o'clock in the morning after downing a half-bottle of wine. (Amy tells us on page 214 that it's really just ordering a gluten free pizza and then dumping heaps of pasta on top and eating it.) But Plato worried about exactly this kind of thing. He believes that our appetitive soul is especially satisfied and nourished by stories like this. We derive a kind of pleasure and enjoyment from stories that appeal to our appetitive desires. Although we might be a little ashamed to publicly announce our own secret bad habits, we lower our guard against hearing Amy's. Plato tells us:

> If there are any jokes that you yourself would be ashamed to tell but that you very much enjoy hearing and don't detest as something evil in comic plays or in private, aren't you doing the same as in the case of what provokes pity? The part of you that wanted to tell the jokes and that was held back by reason, for fear of being thought a buffoon, you then release, not realizing that, by making it strong in this way, you will be led into becoming a figure of fun where your own affairs are concerned. (*Republic*, 606c1–8)

Plato worried that by repeatedly indulging in the appetitive part of our soul, we lower our guards against keeping them in check in our own lives. Eventually, we *become* our favorite characters in our guiltiest pleasures, which is bad for the soul. Essentially, we become worse humans by humoring ourselves with stories of people whose souls aren't in order.

Schumer, much more forgiving of human flaws, says:

> We all have habits we don't want people to know about. Most are fairly harmless, but we still keep them a secret because we feel like we should. Some people only eat fast food in secret, and some people, like my sister-in-law, watch reality TV that is so trashy it should be illegal. How do I know that? Because I watch it right there with her and make her watch even worse TV. Some people like to eat the inside stuffing of their couch. Only God can judge you, brotha! (p. 219)

Amy accepts that human beings are flawed and that we all have embarrassing and unpleasant secrets that we'd rather not share. However, in a rather bold chapter, she publishes her secret bad habits, so they are no longer secrets. What Amy and her contemporaries do is to carve out a space for female representation that has been long allotted to men—

a morally ambiguous, sometimes unlikable and messy female anti-hero.

Of course, Plato recognized the talents and capabilities of poets and storytellers. What he disputed was the role they played in moral education. In fact, on the "ancient quarrel" between poetry and philosophy, Plato invited the poets to provide their own defense on its benefits. Perhaps on behalf of Amy Schumer, Lena Dunham, the Broad City gals, and Mindy Kaling, we can say that the role of their stories is not to depict characters that exemplify moral virtue, but rather to reflect and explore various aspects of our experience, in this case the female experience.

We might not always want to be like the women we see represented on screen, but we do want to see them being just as complicated as we are.

12
Putting the Fun Back in Non-refundable

ROB LUZECKY

Let's talk about Amy Schumer in *Snatched* (2017). The story of *Snatched* is really quite simple. A woman gets dumped by her loser boyfriend, and she goes on vacation with her mom to Ecuador.

While on vacation, she gets kidnapped, then escapes the clutches of her captors with the help of a cancer patient, who pilots a boat down a river—in a way that's reminiscent of boat trips in far less funny movies like *Apocalypse Now!* (1979) and *The African Queen* (1951). There's a mute, recently retired member of the Special Forces, who seems to like torturing douche-bags. There's a piano teacher who loves his "mama." There's drunken capoeira (Amy's awesome dance moves). There's a tapeworm of magnificent proportions. There's a meeting with the indigenous folk, a zip line trip through the jungle, a nearly-botched rescue, and a reunion with mom (which heralds a resolution of sorts). It's hilarious.

It might be a surprise that the movie didn't do so well with the critics. The movie (at the time of writing) holds a thirty-seven percent approval rating on *Rotten Tomatoes.* (With an approval rating like that, you might think it was directed by Zack Snyder.) Despite this critical drubbing, Amy Schumer's movie is an example of comic genius that involves a profound criticism of Western values.

Despite what some movie critics, analytic philosophers, Ecuadorian kidnappers, and other ne'er-do-wells might proclaim, great comedy and great philosophy are not mutually exclusive categories. Much like a great mother-daughter couple, or the special relationship between a delusional Trader Joe's manager and his bush hat, great comedy and great philosophy go together.

The critical response to *Snatched* shows us some deep problems with how we understand the role of art in society. The movie itself shows us some deep problems with Western moral values, in the sense that all they seem to do is to make us feel bad. By the end of the movie, we find out that sometimes, to have any fun, we have to fundamentally renounce all the negativity that Western society has foisted on us.

So What's with These Critics Dishing All Their Hate?

There have been critics of the arts as long as the arts have existed. The first time that some brave soul walked into her studio (or office, or hovel) and decided to start the ever-so-risky venture of creating art, there was probably someone far less creative and far less daring who set about to writing a scathing critique of that art. Perhaps the first serious art critic was Plato, who, in books Two, Three, and Ten of the *Republic* (not to mention a handful of other dialogues, like the *Sophist* and *Hippias Major*) takes it upon himself to tell us all about the nature of beauty. He thereby sets up a conceptual framework according to which we can criticize art—and Plato includes dramas (such as those we see in the movies) in "art."

Plato thought that the values of a work of art were part of its essence, and that art was essentially a copy of reality. Now as we all know, a copy just isn't as good as the real thing. Seeing a picture postcard of an Ecuadorian waterfall just isn't as good as seeing the actual waterfall. For Plato, the problem with art is that it confuses people by presenting copies of reality, instead of offering us reality.

Now I think we can all agree that, where copies are concerned, some copies are better than others. There are copies with different degrees of worth. A five-year-old can draw a picture that attempts to copy the bed they see before them, and Van Gogh can draw a picture of the bed he sees in front of him. The piece of art that Van Gogh creates is probably a more exact copy of the bed, by which I mean a more accurate representation of the bed. The blue and orange scribble produced by the five-year-old, meanwhile, might not even be recognizable as any piece of furniture I've ever seen.

The basis of Plato's criticism is the specification that *all* art attempts to copy reality, coupled with the acknowledgement that *some* pieces of art are better at copying reality than others. Also, the better pieces of art represent better things. The shitty copies of reality, and the copies of the shitty things within reality, according to Plato, have no place in society. The people who produced those shitty pieces of art had best go looking for another city-state where they can set up their easels.

For Plato, the merits of a work of art are definitely part of the work of art. The beauty of a work of art is a property *of* the work of art, and not a property of some other thing or of our interpretation of the work of art. We moderns might think that Plato's whole concept of the nature of the work of art is just wrong, that beauty is in fact a product of our *judgments* about the work of art. We might think that a judgment about the beauty of a work of art (like a particular movie in which a woman goes on a fun trip to Ecuador with her mom) is a claim about what we *think* of the work of art, and not a statement about what the work of art actually *is*. For us, in our post-post-modern society, beauty is not a property of the work of art, but a statement about us and how we judge works of art.

The Social Determination of Beauty

The Scottish philosopher David Hume (who was writing a couple of thousand years after Plato wanted to kick all the shitty artists out of ancient Athens) was all about the distinction between the properties that belong to a work of art and those that belong to our judgments about a work of art.

In his pretty amazing little essay called "Of the Standard of Taste," Hume makes the case that the value of the work of art is essentially a social determination. When a particular culture decides on the aesthetic value of that scene where Amy's character performs drunken capoeira and knocks another dancer unconscious, the members of that culture are making a statement about their own values.

The great thing about Hume's claim is that it explains why some cultures value a given work of art more highly than other cultures do. (I heard that *Snatched* was a huge hit in Japan and Europe.) To be clear, our judgments of the value, beauty, or goodness of a work of art are thought to be a reflection of what our society values, and not a statement about the artwork itself. For Hume, artworks are the sorts of things that demand that we make value judgments about them, and as long as they do this, they're doing their job.

But who the hell is making these value judgments, and are all of these people right for the job? Hume holds that anybody who beholds a work of art will make a value judgment about it. Anyone who sees *Snatched* will make a value judgment about it. But for Hume, that group of guys who were mildly stoned through the first half of the movie might not be making the *best* determinations about whether the scene where Amy's character coughs up a tapeworm was more hilarious, just as hilarious, or not nearly so hilarious as the scene in which she slammed a shovel into her kidnapper's face.

Hume claims that the people who are most refined—by which we mean, the ones who see the most movies—are the best ones to make claims about whether or not the movie is any good. Hume's theory about aesthetic judgment is wonderfully democratic, in the sense that it recognizes that the value of a movie is determined by everyone who sees a movie, but he also acknowledges that we should let the experts' opinions inform our thoughts on the value of any particular movie.

Do you ever notice that experts tend to be prudes? (They're at least as prudish as half of the men present in the jury room in "12 Angry Men Inside Amy Schumer.") One problem with Hume's claim that we should let the experts decide is that they might decide that a movie is bad *because it offends their moral sensibilities*. Hume recognized this as a possible outcome of his concept of aesthetic value, and he was totally on-board. In a discussion about Greek poetry (which was really just a bunch of shouting in the none-too-pleasant sounding Attic Greek), Hume notes that modern people might really have a problem with the moral messages of some of the poems, and that this really diminishes their value. In other words, Hume acknowledged that some critics might have moral problems with works of art, and he thinks that the works of art *should* be devalued by a society for moral reasons.

The claim that works of art should be devalued for moral reasons is at least as bad as a trip through the Amazon jungle while using a restaurant placemat as a map. There are some scenes in *Snatched* that are bound to run afoul of some people's moral sensibilities. Remember that scene where Amy's character rips the last few pages out of her mom's book? That's really hard to morally justify in a world that values stories with endings, books, and moms. But the problem with saying that a movie is bad *because it upsets our moral sensibilities* might just demonstrate a fundamental misunderstanding of the purpose of art. The problem with saying a movie is bad because it is morally offensive is that perhaps it misses the whole point of some works of art. Art is made to be looked at. Art is made to be talked about. Unlike scissors, harpoon guns, and toilet paper (all of which are designed to be used), art is designed to grab our attention. Some art demands our fixation by vexing us.

Think about Picasso's *Guernica* (1937), or "Football Town Nights" from *Inside Amy Schumer*. They aren't designed to make us feel comfortable. They are designed to upset us. They are designed to offend us on a moral level. Some works of art only come to life as works of art by challenging the moral norms of a culture. That is, there are some artists who create works of art that are designed to make us critically reflect on our own culture's values. These artists seem to want to force us to ask whether the way we look at the world is all that it's cracked up to be. Amy Schumer is one of these artists. Any art critic who condemns a work of art because it upsets his moral sensibilities is just confused about the nature and function of a work of art.

How to Put the "Fun" Back in Your Life

To understand why *Snatched* is such a great comedy, and why Amy Schumer is such a hilarious philosopher, we need to get a quick understanding of some aspects of Friedrich Nietzsche's philosophy.

Nietzsche was one of the funniest guys living alone in an attic apartment in Turin during the late nineteenth century, and he was not at all above dishing the dirt on some of the putatively great figures of Western philosophy and art. He famously referred to Socrates as a physically repulsive, simple-minded criminal. He identified Wagner as a pompous poseur who fell in love with the not-so-great ideas that his characters screamed out over the din of an overly-large orchestra.

Some patently humorless souls have characterized Nietzsche's remarks on Socrates and Wagner as *ad hominem*—a fancy Latin phrase that means "attacking the man"—arguments that should be disregarded. According to them, Nietzsche's philosophy should be dismissed. This might be the case, if all that Nietzsche was doing was trash-talking some people who desperately stood in need of mockery, but in fact, Nietzsche's name-calling was part of a much bigger argument about the very nature of what should and shouldn't be valued.

Nietzsche's fundamental problem with Western values was based on the observation that many of the supposedly best, most moral people were unhappy people who seem to enjoy inflicting unhappiness on others as well. Perhaps looking at that very large group of people who tend to be most vicious and cruel in their application of what they think of as virtuous, Nietzsche observed that they were walking pictures of misery, constantly at war with everyone, in the sense that they are always busy telling anyone who was not quick enough to plug their ears about all the things that they should do in order to be a good person. And as if this weren't bad enough, these moralizers also seem to take great joy in promptly telling everyone within earshot about why they should feel *guilty* for failing to live up to all of the unrealizable ideals of what a person should be.

We see a great example of this right at the start of *Snatched*, in the scene in which Amy's character (Emily) is busy shopping for clothes for her upcoming vacation. As one customer storms out of the store, Emily's boss not-so-gently reprimands her for shopping instead of selling clothes. The thing that is remarkable about this scene is that, right after receiving the reprimand, Amy's character expresses no guilt. Sure, she comes up with various excuses attempting to justify her actions. She comes up with reasons for not being huddled in some back room folding clothes, so that soccer-moms and other consumers can feel good about plunking down some cash for a piece of pastel-colored cotton. But she does not say "sorry". In fact, Amy's character expresses indignation when she's fired. As she jauntily puts on her hat, Amy's character happily walks out of the store seeking a new adventure. By the end of the scene, the only person who's unhappy is the boss, who recognizes that she is the appointed arbiter of the bullshit values imposed on her by an impersonal corporate system.

One of Nietzsche's most brilliant psychological insights is based on the observation that feeling bad is not natural. In the second essay of his *On the Genealogy of Morals*, Nietzsche asks why most societies, all through history, located in incredibly diverse parts of the planet—places as far flung as Ecuador, Rome, China, Greece, and the UK—seem to dedicate themselves to finding better ways to torture people, beat them up, and basically make them feel all sorts of physical pain.

Nietzsche concludes that the purpose of all this imposed suffering is to make people internalize their pain. That is, societies try to make people feel that their choices are what caused them to feel like shit. The terrible trick that societies pulled on people was convincing them that they were responsible for their pain. When Nietzsche points out that all of our negativity has been beaten into us, he is specifying that it is absolutely not natural.

The question is, why make a bunch of people always feel bad, always question themselves, about everything they have ever done or thought of doing? For Nietzsche, the answer is as simple as it is scary (at least as scary as a foot-long tapeworm). If we go around all mopey and riven with self-doubt, then there is far more chance that we will just accept the values present in our society. The shittier the members of a culture feel, the less rebellious they will be.

Throughout *Snatched*, Amy's character continually demonstrates that we shouldn't feel so bad about the things that Western society wants to make us feel bad about. Think about Amy's character's speech (to her mother) in the first few minutes of the movie: There she is, proudly wearing a brilliant cat-themed shirt while she stands beside a hideous sculpture of the cat in her mom's living-room. Moments before, she discovered an old photo album that contains pictures of her mom smiling, laughing joyously in front of amazing landmarks like the Eiffel Tower and the Palace of Westminster. Van Morrison's beautiful "Madam George" plays in the background, and Amy's character realizes that, once upon a time, her mom used to do more with her life than internet-stalk her daughter, cook meals for her man-boy son, and go to sculpting class to make unnaturally proportioned and altogether upsetting statues of cats.

Armed with the photo album and the knowledge that her mom used to be awesome, Amy cajoles her mom into joining her on the trip to Ecuador. Amy's mom shoots back that her knees can't take it, and that she is too old, and that you can't go on a trip without at least two years' planning. Every reason not to go on the trip is an expression of the negativity that Western society has told her that she should feel. Amy's character knows that as long as her mom—or any of us—parrot that negativity, no one will ever put the "fun" back in any non-refundable trip, or anything else for that matter.

In demanding that her mom come on the trip, Linda, Emily, and (hopefully) we the members of the audience discover that feeling bad all the time is not something we need to do. This is a profound critique of Western values, in the sense that the movie affirms human potential. The moral message of the movie is that you can break up with your loser boyfriend, you can get shit-faced drunk and dance with your tit hanging out, you can go on vacation with your mom, and it will be awesome.

You can navigate through a jungle with a restaurant placemat for a map and discover that your mom is a pretty awesome person to have by your side. You even discover that your brother, who's agoraphobic, can (kind of) lead a team of US commandos. Throughout it all, you discover that, despite all the negativity beat into you by your culture, you do not yet know all of the things you can do. And most of the things you think you can't do (and all the negatively that is associated with those things) might be just as fabricated as the bush-cap on the head of an all-too-stressed-out Trader Joe's manager.

IV

Women Are Funny

13 The Laughter and the Fury

LEIGH KOLB

The first episode of *Inside Amy Schumer* (2013) lays it all out on the casting couch. In "2 Girls, 1 Cup," Amy Schumer, in character, goes to a casting call and listens to a male director give graphic descriptions of the acting job—lesbian action, human excrement back and forth—surely an instant classic (because, well, it actually was).

Amy takes the shock in stride and quickly resigns herself to the job for the screen time. The catch (besides the non-simulated scat porn) is that Amy must lose weight for the role. She jokes that maybe she'll just lose it the day of—in the cup. The director grows serious, and her co-star pauses over her takeout. He scolds her: "That's gross, Amy. She's eating."

Amy is receiving and illustrating the clear message: you can't win. But you're going to have to try, and it's going to be miserable. The expectation to contort and perform for the male gaze, no questions asked, is the norm. The woman sitting beside her is afforded some kind of dignity due to her thinness and conventional beauty. And when Amy tries to use humor to self-deprecate, she's chastised.

Inside Amy Schumer exists in the present context of postfeminist backlash and raunch culture, in a society that still deeply holds to ancient notions of both women's roles and women's perfection. The postfeminist backlash comes whenever there is even a threat that women will achieve equality;

for every feminist action, there's an opposite and misogynistic reaction. "Raunch culture," so named by Ariel Levy in *Female Chauvinist Pigs*, attempts to convince young women that their empowerment can be found in front of *Girls Gone Wild* cameras, and not in the pages of Simone de Beauvoir. Thrashing against the gains of feminism, a postfeminist landscape relies on deeply embedded historical misogyny to keep the backlashes coming.

In Aristotle's *Poetics*, he makes this declaration: "valor in a woman, or unscrupulous cleverness is inappropriate." But he also maintains the idea that "character must be true to life" (*Poetics*, I.XV). This contradicts his classic and permeating argument that, "the male is by nature superior and the female inferior, the male ruler and the female subject" (*Politics,* I.V). Taking all of these ideas together makes it impossible to imagine true female representation. Woman is by nature inferior, and in drama—which should reflect reality—woman should not be brave or clever. While Aristotle saw *mimesis* (meaning, "imitation" or "mimicry" of nature and individuals) as fundamental to *human* expression, this integral practice of art, literature, drama and comedy has long been relegated to the representation of only the *male* experience.

Over two thousand years after Aristotle made his gendered decrees, French philosopher Hélène Cixous wrote "The Laugh of the Medusa," an essay that demands women reclaim and rewrite their lives, rejecting the millennia of silencing at the hands of patriarchal systems. Conjuring the image of the Medusa, the monstrous woman of Greek mythology whose rejection of celibacy turned her blonde hair to snakes and her beauty to destructive power, Cixous suggests that women must reject and re-examine the mythologies of the past to write the true reality of women's lives. Cixous writes, "A feminine text cannot fail to be more than subversive . . . There's no room for her if she's not a he. If she's a her-she, it's in order to smash everything, to shatter the framework of institutions, to blow up the law, to break up the 'truth' with laughter." French philosopher Luce Irigaray argues that *mimesis*, as a "process of resubmitting women to stereotypical views of women in order to call the views themselves into question" is a powerful tool.

The arc of human social thought is not constantly forward-moving. Cixous and Irigaray wrote their visions in the 1970s, and we see *Inside Amy Schumer* following those theoretical foundations. However, we also see bubbling to the surface a resurgence of anti-feminism in the force of "postfeminism," which makes feminism unpalatable to young women. In "A Rather Crude Feminism," Jason Middleton uses Angela McRobbie's notions of postfeminism to build an argument for the power of *Inside Amy Schumer*. McRobbie says that post-feminist culture "makes feminism quite unpalatable to young women (the words repulsive and disgusting are often used)." Middleton adds that "patriarchal power is sustained . . . by securing the consent and participation of young women." Rejecting feminism leads to accepting patriarchy.

It is within these realms that *Inside Amy Schumer* exists: the historical, male-centric storytelling that was demanded in ancient Greek thought and that has continued to permeate Western culture, the liberal and radical feminists of the 1970s whose rhetoric attempts to change the narrative, and the pushback of twenty-first-century postfeminist raunch culture. Situating itself in this historical and cultural context, *Inside Amy Schumer*, starting with an uncomfortable and satirical look at the disgust and impossibility of the casting couch—where all of these forces collide—has spent four seasons (so far) breaking up truth with laughter through *mimesis* and social commentary that cuts to the core of destructive postfeminism.

Do You Think I'm a Monster?

Women have been pushed, prodded, and excluded from meaningful representation throughout history; they are relegated to the private sphere of the home (*oikos*), instead of the masculine space of the public sphere (*polis*). (Surprise: this also was Aristotle's ideology and is one that has permeated Western culture, taking hold especially during and since industrialization.) Male thinkers' decrees and mythologies have long silenced or distorted women's stories, relying upon fear and a desire to keep the social order of female subjugation.

In *Women and Laughter*, Frances Gray points out:

> Women, in the face of all the odds, have always contrived to create laughter, in private and in public, as artists and as social beings. Feminism, however, has only just begun to engage with laughter as a social force; it is now an urgent matter to provide a body of theory if female laughter is not to continue to be read in the light of definitions which at worst deny its very existence and at best force it into specifically masculine moulds.

Irigaray's theory that *mimesis* has the power to subject audiences to the ludicrousness of patriarchal subjugation and female stereotypes can be seen throughout *Inside Amy Schumer*.

In "I'm So Bad," a group of women are out to eat, sharing stories that end with them confessing, "I'm so bad." The moral badness they are referring to, though, has to do with what they've eaten. They preface their food confessions with actual moral and ethical failings (cyberbullying, not helping a suicidal woman, an abortion so late-term that there's not a word for it, and animal cruelty). At the end of the sketch, they sheepishly agree to share a dessert, but then violently attack the waiter, clawing apart and eating his face. One woman, however—who has been quiet during the confessions—stays at the table and calmly and confidently orders flan.

There are a number of sketches throughout the series that all contain a similar trajectory of satirizing sociocultural stereotypes of women and ending violently (with the exception of the woman who doesn't participate in the expected behavior). In "I'm So Bad," "Compliments," "Can I Stand in My Truth?" and "Better for the Baby," female characters—through Irigaray's methodology of using *mimesis* to disrupt stereotypes—perform in ways that are both stereotypical and familiar.

The twisted morality of "I'm So Bad" highlights how women are conditioned to believe eating poorly and being overweight are their worst moral failings. "Compliments" shows how women feel they must reject compliments. "Can I Stand in My Truth?" makes it apparent that women are allowed only to fantasize about their dreams (opening a bakery in Maine). In the sketch that shows pregnant women bragging about their alternative birth plans, Schumer shows the all-too-real competition that exists surrounding pregnancy and birth. In each of these sketches, the woman who eschews the satirical stereotype—who eats the dessert, accepts the compliment, actually does open a bakery, or elects to trust her doctor—is safe and content, while the others who act out the stereotypes have violent and horrifying ends.

Cixous says, "Men have committed the greatest crime against women. Insidiously, violently, they have led them to hate other women, to be their own enemies." This is another way in which patriarchy keeps its hold: it convinces women that there's only so much power to compete for, convinces them to hate themselves, and convinces them to compete with women and see other women as the enemy. This keeps women both distracted and destructive in a society that needs their feminine power to be strong and collaborative. Sketches like "Judging Strippers" and "Cool with It" illustrate this notion further.

We know that women were long shut out of the dignity that true representation affords. They have been expected to be moral and virtuous, but not intelligent or clever. They have been expected to be perfect in largely superficial ways, but not allowed to be fully human through the complexities that public life and intellectual inquiry allow. These sketches illustrate that being thrust from patriarchal confines to the internalized misogyny of postfeminism leads women into superficial and damaging situations that offer no clear way out. Striving for this kind of perfection can only end in monstrous destruction.

You Are Gorgeous No Matter What You Do

The obsession with female perfection (even as women have historically been shut out of the institutions of public life, political leadership and education, while conversely being denied respect and dignity) infiltrates the social movements that have arisen out of patriarchal systems. Anti-feminists (of course) demand the aforementioned impossibilities from women. However, even liberal feminism often holds the bar quite high for what it means to be a feminist (see Roxane Gay's collection of essays, *Bad Feminist*). The aforementioned sketches eviscerate cultural expectations, but they also turn a mirror to this kind of liberal feminism that demands it all.

Women are held to standards of perfection that are illogical and unobtainable. One way that twenty-first-century raunch culture and postfeminism have embodied and twisted this ideal is by inflating self-esteem to a dangerous peak of entitlement and a destructive lack of empathy. In the episode, "Psychopath Test," Amy and her girlfriends perform a song that celebrates this kind of bastardized perfection. Opening with the seemingly innocuous line: "You are gorgeous no matter what you do," we're faced with a familiar female-empowerment anthem. You are gorgeous, you are perfect, you are beautiful just the way you are. The reality of this kind of faux empowerment, though, is faulty and dangerous. If you are perfect and beautiful, confident and strong—as girls and women are taught to be in a culture that makes it impossible to believe—then you can do no wrong. This sketch asks what happens when women hear those fake messages of empowerment and take them to their limit?

"Claim a miscarriage when no pregnancy occurred / Or do a karaoke rap so you can scream the N-word / Follow your heart and swing for the fences / Fellate your friend's husband, the only consequence is / You are so beautiful!" The DJ later interjects, "Keep your chin held high and your empathy nonexistent."

The *mimesis* in this sketch—it sounds like it could easily be a "girl power" anthem—serves to shock the viewer with the actual lyrics. There's a forced realization that this kind of superficial self-esteem and self-centeredness again makes women monstrously turn against themselves and one another through the illusion of perfection. If society doesn't give me the dignity of complexity or listen to my truth, and generations of subjugation have led to a kind of faux empowerment (that still typically centers itself around beauty)—then I should be able to do whatever I want.

In the *New Yorker*, Emily Nussbaum writes (of Schumer's recurring characterization of the kind of "monstrous" woman): "she's smart but self-destructive, the sadder-but-wiser girl, who knows how easily desperation can masquerade as freedom. This self-mockery could turn into masochism, but somehow it never does, in part because the sharpness of the jokes is itself a form of self-assertion." Schumer's ability to employ *mimesis* to break up the "truth" with laughter is sharp and subversive, and desperately needed. Cixous says that "writing is precisely *the very possibility of change*, the space that can serve as a springboard for subversive thought, the precursory movement of a transformation of social and cultural structures." Schumer (along with her writing team) has consistently been subversive, with the clear goal of transforming how women and men think about the social and cultural structures that confine them.

You're the Coach Who Don't Like Rapin'

Schumer doesn't only satirize female performances and sociocultural expectations. *Inside Amy Schumer* unabashedly turns that mirror toward men as well. Cixous claims that men rely upon "cultural orthopedics," which include an entertainment media that has long been created by them and for them, which of course has roots in ancient Greek drama also being by them and for them. Schumer's mere presence as a female-led, feminist sketch comedy show on Comedy Central—a largely male space—takes away some of that masculine comfort.

The "entitlement machine" that we see in media that caters to the male gaze, to rape culture, to legislation that strips women of bodily autonomy, must be challenged. "Football Town Nights," a spoof on the TV high-school football drama *Friday Night Lights*, takes on rape culture. The town's new football coach has a new mantra for his team: "Clear eyes, full hearts, don't rape" (a play on the *Friday Night Lights* motto, "Clear eyes, full hearts, can't lose"). The teenage boys protest and beg; however, they are not the only ones. The townspeople—from elderly women to parents—are disgusted with the new coach's restrictions.

While this sketch would have been brilliant had it ended with that commentary, the final monologue that the coach delivers takes the point and doubles down. He assures them that they can play football without raping, because this is what football is really about: "It's about violently dominating anyone that stands between you and what you want! You gotta get yourself into the mindset that you are gods, and you are entitled to this!" This isn't just about teen boys. It's not about football. It's about American culture and the male dominance and entitlement that permeates it.

Inside Amy Schumer features numerous sketches that hold up what at first seems like a distorted funhouse mirror, but isn't. In "A Very Realistic Military Game," Amy attempts to play a military shooter game with her boyfriend, and she chooses a female soldier avatar who is sexually assaulted and must go through the laborious and shaming process of reporting the assault. Online forums and her boyfriend dismiss her difficulties, saying that means that perhaps she shouldn't play. "Lunch at O'Nutters" satirizes the Hooters franchise, with waiters' bulging packages in tight shorts and female coworkers trying to boost a male coworker's mood after a breakup by taking him there (he ends up dancing on the table and enjoying the pitchers of pinot grigio).

In "Birth Control," Amy must ask permission from numerous men before getting a birth control prescription filled, but a young boy gets a gun from the pharmacist who tells him it's his right. "Madonna vs. Whore" takes us in the bedroom of a couple who are sleeping together for the first time; the man wants Amy to be sexually experienced, but not too much. She contorts herself and tries to fit his impossible expectations—and after they have sex, asks with bewilderment, "Did I come?" And in "Milk Milk Lemonade," a hip hop anthem with a bevy of booty shorts and popping asses, the women rap, "This is where my poop comes out / This is what you think is hot."

The premise of these sketches seems ludicrous. But after the laughter subsides what remains is this: this is exactly what you [men] are doing. This is exactly what happens. The conceptual orthopedics are loosened; the gears to the entitlement machine slow.

She's Built Like a Lineman and She Has Cabbage Patch-like Features. Her Ass Makes Me Furious

Contrasted with the agreeable Amy (who needed to build her résumé in "2 Girls 1 Cup"), Amy Schumer's real-life and on-screen personas shot to stardom as the show increased in popularity. For stars—especially women—this typically has consequences, as the need for and impossibility of female perfection is demanded at higher decibels. Nussbaum says that "there's a risk to Schumer's rise—when you're put on a pedestal, the whole world gets to upskirt you. Now comes the hype, the lash and the backlash, and the backlash to the backlash . . . It's happened again and again to the new wave of female TV creators." While she was vocal in her struggles with this, Schumer wrote herself into the show with honesty.

Season Two opens with "Focus Group," in which men are asked to critique the comedy of *Inside Amy Schumer*. Instead, they objectify and criticize Schumer herself. We think we're getting a breath of fresh air when a man says that he enjoyed the on-the-street interviews and that the show had a "feminist bent," but he adds that he would have enjoyed it more if Schumer had a "ten percent better dumper." When asked to rate the show's comedy between one and ten, the men wrote, "not bang her," "would bang her," and one just drew a picture of boobs. Behind a two-way mirror, Schumer says, "A couple of them said they would bang me?" and smiles at the camera. This—like so many of the sketches—would have been powerful enough without the clincher at the end. The criticism that Schumer receives from men is often rooted in objectification and her lack of what they consider to be perfect female attributes. However, she figuratively winks at the camera at the end, showing us the honesty of what it might feel like to be above the animalistic criticism but still hungry for approval.

Schumer consistently takes the criticism she receives and observes, and she turns it into thoughtful and scathing commentary on society as a whole. Her confidence in doing so grows throughout the seasons. In Season Three, Schumer creates an ambitious and critically acclaimed whole-episode sketch: "12 Angry Men Inside Amy Schumer." A parody of the classic *12 Angry Men* play and movie, the jurors must deliberate whether or not Amy Schumer is hot enough to be on TV. At first, there's only one voice that says "yes," but the arguments mount to prove whether there is enough evidence that she could give the men a "reasonable chub." Schumer wrote the sketch based on some real insults she's received, and in the broader vein of what female stars have to deal with that men do not ("I don't think she's protagonist hot . . ." / "But Kevin James is?"). The writing, directing, and acting are brilliant. One of the most noteworthy aspects of the episode is how angry the men become in their deliberations. Her confidence and her audacity to be a protagonist who doesn't fit their mold make them furious.

In Season Four's "New Twitter Button," Schumer again revisits that same kind of rage that reveals itself on social media. As a shortcut for male users who have to spend too much time writing their threats against women online, Twitter unveils a new "I'm Going to Rape and Kill You" button. The Twitter spokesperson says, "What's the point of using the anonymity of the Internet to just call someone fat when you can also make them feel physically threatened?" She goes on to sell the feature, explaining that this frees up more characters for men to tell women "what ugly sluts they are." Exposing this rage is again holding up that mirror that appears to distort reality, but instead is just reality; and in doing so, Schumer again breaks apart the truths that must be faced.

In an interview about "12 Angry Men Inside Amy Schumer," Schumer addresses what it was like to write the insults about herself:

> I'm just sitting there and coming up with new ways to trash myself. Once we were shooting it, and once we were in the room, it was not hurtful at all. It's very liberating, actually. It's also because I *am* confident, I am someone who feels comfortable in my own skin, and I do feel sexy. But I also know that opinion is out there about me. I honestly, eventually, didn't take it personally at all. But when I was first sitting there writing it, to write thirty-plus pages, where on every page, it's everything that could be wrong with you, and all these different reasons why people would say, "You shouldn't be someone who's looked at," yeah, it was a bummer. But then it became really fun and liberating, and I'm so proud of what we turned it into. And I think it was good for me. (*Uproxx*, 2015)

In addressing the broader rage that is displayed in "12 Angry Men Inside Amy Schumer," she says: "it's a behavior I want to point out in people. Just examine it for them. Hopefully, people recognize behavior in themselves. And I also think it's funny."

This comment, which can be applied to many of Schumer's sketches (the combination of serious social commentary and playful humor) reinforces the power of her comedy, and the reason for the pushback from fictional jurors and real-life trolls. Cixous says that "Smug-faced readers, managing editors, and big bosses don't like the true texts of women—female-sexed texts. That kind scares them." The fear of women writing and speaking their truths results in fear, which all too often results in backlash and rage. How dare she?

The Laughing Medusa, Sponsored by Sea Spray

In Schumer's comedy, the complexities and impossibilities of societal expectations and internalized misogyny are often laid bare. She wants people to recognize themselves in order to effect change, and she also thinks these observations are simply funny. There are many scenarios, however, that end with violence (self-inflicted or otherwise), which shows how impossible a solution seems.

In all of Schumer's sketches about female stereotypes regarding behavior and competition, women ultimately destroy themselves or one another if they fall into the traps of delusion. In "I'm Sorry," women scientists stumble over one another apologizing for others' misdeeds. When a woman's legs are severed from hot coffee that a man spilled, she is faultless but cannot stop apologizing. This popular sketch exposed the habitual apologizing that we have come to expect from women. It's not that we shouldn't ever apologize (as shown in the "You Are Gorgeous" music video), but what we're doing leaves us falling all over one another, crumpled up on the floor and useless. We all see ourselves in these scenes—and question while we laugh.

Cixous says that women live in a place of guilt: "guilty of everything, guilty at every turn: for having desires, for not having any; for being frigid, for being 'too hot': for not being both at once; for being too motherly and not enough; for having children and for not having any; for nursing and for not nursing . . ." This place of impossible guilt and inner conflict can feel insurmountable, and Schumer's sketches that end in the female subjects' self-destruction—and exploding heads—illustrate that kind of confounding dilemma.

In "Gang Bang," Amy—as a proud feminist—stages an amateur porn shoot; she will be starring in a gang bang to "prove that women are not objects." This premise, plus the fact that she can barely name feminists who came before, show her grasp on feminism is shaky at best (which can be said about too many people in the postfeminist landscape).

She's taken aback that the men who show up—who physically disappoint her—aren't that into her, either. One of the men challenges her feminism because she seems to want to be objectified, and her head explodes. A book titled *Stories of Feminist Bravery, Sponsored by Sea Spray* (Amy's cranberry juice of choice to avoid UTIs) appears on screen, with portraits of Susan B. Anthony, Abigail Adams, and Eleanor Roosevelt, whose heads also explode. This image also reappears at the very end of the Season Four finale, "Rubbing Our Clips."

The "horror" of postfeminism is that this sustained patriarchal power coupled with raunch culture and a rejection of feminism for the trade-off of faux empowerment destroys women. Time and again, Schumer's sketches suggest that her characters—who embody the horrors of postfeminism—could be saved by feminism.

Schumer pushes boundaries and demands much more than laughter in her groundbreaking sketch series. By placing complex and cringe-worthy women's stories front and center, and sharply cutting the culture of masculine entitlement, she succeeds in ridiculing realities and expectations that are too often left uncriticized.

Inside Amy Schumer gives us proud bodies and loud revolts. We may not be perfect, but we will no longer be quiet—nor will we be forced to eat the excrement of postfeminism.

14
Five Stereotypes that Sustain Grape Zones

MICHELLE CIURRIA

In her autobiography and recent interviews, Amy Schumer talks about "grape," the grey area between rape and consensual sex. She associates grape with certain encounters, such as "the guy you went home with in college, and you said, 'No,' and then he still did it, or maybe you woke up and it was someone you were dating" (NPR, 2013).

She also discusses her experience of waking up to find her first boyfriend having sex with her, and then continuing to date him, unsure if he had done anything wrong. (Years later, she realized that it was rape). Grape can take many forms, but the paradigm case is when a woman isn't sure whether she's been raped, because her experience doesn't match dominant cultural stereotypes about so-called "real rape."

How does grape happen? How is there uncertainty about whether a sex act counts as rape? There is no doubt that we as a culture have difficulty identifying and prosecuting rape. According to Jane Kim's article, "Taking Rape Seriously: Rape as Slavery," most rapes are not reported, and of those reported, 84 percent are not prosecuted. These statistics explain why people describe our society as a "rape culture," in which rape is both endemic and normalized. Grape zones are a critical part of this culture: they disguise acts of rape as innocent and inevitable.

To explain grape zones, we must refer to pervasive stereotypes that normalize rape. These stereotypes make it difficult for us to recognize non-consensual sex acts as rape when those acts do not conform to recognizable archetypes. This situation creates grape zones, or gaps in our shared cultural knowledge about rape. These gaps in turn prevent us, as a culture, from easily identifying, responding to, and prosecuting rape. In philosophical terms, grape zones are instances of what Miranda Fricker calls "hermeneutical gaps." Hermeneutical gaps are holes in our shared knowledge that prevent us from understanding and appreciating the experiences of historically disenfranchised groups—women, racialized minorities, the poor, rape survivors, and so on. Grape zones occur when there are bundles of stereotypical assumptions about rape survivors, rapists, and contexts in which rape can and cannot occur, which create gaps in our shared knowledge about rape. Because of these gaps in our shared knowledge, it becomes difficult for us to recognize rape in all of its forms.

There is good news and bad news. The bad news is that grape zones are everywhere, because cultural stereotypes about rape are pervasive. On an individual level, these stereotypes give rise to *implicit biases* against rape survivors who don't match our common assumptions about who can and can't be raped—about who is "rapeable." (By "rapeable," I mean credible as a rape victim, according to the popular imagination; hence, women who are seen as "unrapeable" are stereotyped as invulnerable to sexual violence, and as such, their testimony about sexual violence is regarded as untrustworthy or incredible). And when I use the term "victim," I mean to refer to someone who has experienced sexual violence. There are extensive debates about whether "victim," "survivor," or "victim-survivor" is the preferable term, but I will simply use "victim," with the caveat that victims are agents capable of survival and autonomous choice, though they have experienced an injurious human rights violation.

Implicit biases are unconscious stereotypical assumptions of which we are not fully aware. Even if we try very hard, we cannot always identify our implicit states, because they're part of the unconscious mind. Thus, when we're considering whether a scenario counts as rape, we're liable to draw on a store of implicit biases without even realizing it. The good news is that we can exercise *indirect* control over our implicit biases by critically examining the cultural stereotypes that underpin and reinforce them. By scrutinizing stereotypes about rape, we can gain control over the corresponding implicit biases in our unconscious minds. More specifically, we can gain the ability to withhold, suppress, and perhaps even extinguish these biases.

A Schumerian Representation of Bias

Schumer presents an extreme example of implicit bias in a sketch from her TV show called "Football Town Nights," which is a parody of *Friday Night Lights*. The local football team is meeting a new coach, who is introducing a radical new policy of *not raping*. The football players are shocked and appalled, and immediately start rattling off common putative excuses for rape, which draw on the cultural stereotype of the "guilty victim": what if she was dressed sexy, was drunk, had a reputation for promiscuity, or said "yes" at an earlier time (to something else)? The football players cannot disentangle cultural stereotypes about sex (which misrepresent rape as consensual) from actual consensual sex. The sketch is effective, because it intermingles these familiar excuses with patently absurd ones, such as, "What if she's dressed as a sexy ghost?," and "What if my mom is the District Attorney and definitely won't prosecute?" These ridiculous excuses reduce to absurdity the more familiar but equally illegitimate ones, highlighting the irrationality of *all* rape defenses. This is a comedy sketch with some serious philosophical reasoning.

The football players' excuses rest mainly on false stereotypes about gender and female sexual purity. Unfortunately, these stereotypes are often invoked in real-life court cases and still play a role in popular culture, as we shall see.

Schumer does a great job of demonstrating the absurdity of these stereotypes in her show. There are at least five stereotypes that create grape zones which support rape culture:

1. **the stereotype of the "stranger rapist," lurking in bushes and back alleys, which biases us against marital, date, and acquaintance rape—by far the most common types of rape;**
2. **the stereotype of the "sexually pure," "chaste," and conventionally feminine rape victim, which biases us against victims who have unconventional sexual traits and preferences;**
3. **the stereotype that rape always involves physical force or violence, which biases us against incapacitated and immobilized rape victims;**
4. **the stereotype that rapists are poor, racialized (non-white), and uneducated, which protects all the white, rich, educated rapists from fair and proportional sentencing;**
5. **the stereotype that rape can't happen to a "strong-ass woman" like Amy Schumer** (*The Girl With the Lower Back Tattoo,* p. 183).

By debunking these stereotypes, we reduce the influence of grape on our judgments, and also shrink the scope of grape zones in our culture. By critically evaluating implicitly-held stereotypes, we start to become a hell of a lot more clear on what rape is. By discussing grape and rape, Schumer is demonstrating that nobody, never, not ever, is "unrapeable" or even "ungrapeable." The notion of the "ideal victim" needs to be debunked.

Stranger Danger

We're all familiar with the stereotype of the stranger rapist. In a famous scene in Stanley Kubrick's film *A Clockwork Or-*

ange, Alex breaks into a random house and theatrically rapes a woman in front of her husband. Not only is this an example of stranger rape, it also tacitly draws on the coverture law of the nineteenth century, in which a woman had no legal rights or entitlements independently of her husband. Alex's sick and violent actions clearly violated the woman, but the protagonist's act of sexual violence is presented as a slight to the husband.

Coverture was a legal doctrine that held throughout most of the nineteenth century, stating that a woman's rights are subsumed under those of her husband. Although the law was abolished in the nineteenth century, it continued to influence Western culture, which did not grant women the right to vote or participate in civic life until the early twentieth century.

The patriarchal history of the Western legal system helps to explain why marital rape was not criminalized in all American states until 1993, and why the phrase "date rape" did not enter the popular lexicon or legal vernacular until feminist journalist Susan Brownmiller named it in her popular 1975 book, *Against Our Will*. As a result, for most of the twentieth century, marital rape and date rape were not understood as rape *per se*. There were no shared discursive frameworks or legal apparatuses for describing, understanding, or identifying these acts *as rape*, or even as harmful. This is not to say that these violations did not occur—they most certainly did. But they were not publicly recognized as rape, as harmful, as criminal, or as oppressive to women as a class.

Although such concepts as acquaintance rape and marital rape are now public knowledge, both have been less widely recognized than stranger rape, and thus they continue to be widely misunderstood. In *Gone with the Wind*, Rhett Butler rapes Scarlett O'Hara, and yet this scene has been acclaimed as one of the most romantic gestures in Hollywood cinema. In *Grease*—a movie rated as suitable for a general audience—Danny Zuko brags that his girlfriend Sandy Olsson "put up a fight" when they had sex, and his friends congratulate him. In *Lolita* (both the book and the two film adaptations), Humbert Humbert rapes and psychologically abuses his twelve-year-old stepdaughter, and yet *Vanity Fair* extols the rapist's first-person narrative as, "the only convincing love story of our century." (This appears as a blurb on the cover of the Everyman's Library hardcover edition.) In fact, *Lolita* exemplifies two poorly understood types of sex crime: acquaintance rape and statutory rape. Evidently, the average twentieth-century moviegoer did not recognize acquaintance rape, partner rape, or statutory rape as prosecutable sex crimes. These stereotypes die hard.

The archetype of the stranger rapist continues to divert attention and resources away from the non-stereotypical rapes that are far more prevalent. According to *The National Intimate Partner and Sexual Violence Survey*, fewer than 10 percent of rapes are perpetrated by strangers; partner and acquaintance rape account for 50 and 40 percent of rapes, respectively. The social archetype of the stranger rapist makes it difficult for victims to prosecute the majority of sexual offenses.

The Heteronormative, Cisgender Victim

The stereotypical "legitimate rape victim" is a cisgender heterosexual woman—a virgin or a wife. This schema can again be traced back to the legal doctrine of coverture, according to which a wife's legal rights and obligations are to be controlled by her husband. Unmarried women, presumed to be virgins, could be harmed by rape in the sense that they could be damaged and therefore rendered unmarriageable. Unmarried women who were sexually active were already deemed unmarriageable, so they could not be harmed by rape in a way that society recognized. Gender non-conforming women had low marriage prospects in the cis-heteronormative economy, so they, too, were deemed less amenable to sexual injury, since "injury" was a function of marriageability.

The (stupid) idea is that if someone is not harmed by non-consensual sex, then it does not count as "rape," and the only kind of "harm" that counts is a reduction to one's chances of marriage. Married women, too, could not be *legally* raped by their husbands. The only "real rape" was rape perpetrated by a man on a cis-heterosexual woman who was either a virgin or someone else's wife. Most women were "unrapeable," according to the law and social conventions of the time.

The whole idea of a woman's "marriageability" no longer makes sense, of course, and even when it was a popular notion, in reality it was a myth that served to reinforce patriarchal relations and to disguise them as natural and necessary. Yet even today, women who are not straight and cisgender are seen as less rapeable, even though they are more often raped. According to *The Human Rights Campaign,* bisexual women and transgender women, who do not conform to feminine sexual conventions, are raped in higher numbers than heterosexual, cisgender women, but their testimony is often seen as less credible than others'.

Women who engage in non-standard sexual practices (like BDSM) are also at risk of being stigmatized and falsely discredited. In 2016 and 2017, musician and CBC host Jian Ghomeshi was charged with seven counts of sexual assault, which he defended as consensual BDSM, even though the defendants all denied that consent was given. He was later acquitted on grounds of insufficient evidence. There is a lesson here. When women are thought to have engaged in non-standard sexual practices, they can be seen as less credible in the eyes of society and the law, and these practices can also be invoked to disguise sexual violence as consensual. These excuses are often accepted in court, because they rest on popular stereotypes that depict gender non-conforming women as "unrapeable."

In Schumer's *Leather Special* on Netflix, she dresses in a tight, black, leather bodysuit, which our culture associates with female sexuality, bondage, and domination. This wardrobe choice is somewhat ironic, given that Schumer proceeds to compare the outfit disparagingly to a "Glad garbage bag," to liken her sexual performance to the stiff movements of a silver street performer, and to embrace the fact that she is, according to the media, "fat" but "brave."

While the monologue might appear to be self-effacing at first blush, its real purpose is to challenge conventional assumptions about what kind of woman can be a sexual agent. Schumer is effectively saying that cultural conventions be damned—a fat, funny, outgoing, smart-ass woman can be just as sexual, and as sexy, as anyone else. But then, is it so hard to believe that a gender non-conforming woman could also have been raped? Schumer breaks down outdated stereotypes about the credibility of rape victims, and stale archetypes of female sexuality, in the same hilarious (but ingeniously calculated) stroke.

The upshot is that whether rape has occurred or not depends on only one factor: whether affirmative consent was given. The victim's sexual identity is beside the point.

The Resisting Victim

Historically, rape laws defined rape as involving the use of *physical* force, though US laws in most jurisdictions have since been amended to include other types of forcible compulsion, such as having sex with an incapacitated person. Nonetheless, judges can give harsher sentences for rape when physical force is used. This provision can bias people against victims who were unconscious and victims who did not physically resist their assailant, even though this is a natural response to violence for many people. Recent research has shown that rape victims can experience temporary paralysis or "tonic immobility," preventing them from resisting assault.

The popular myth that rape victims always aggressively fight back is based on an out-dated model of human psychology, on which fight-or-flight mechanisms are triggered in response to perceived danger. In fact, responses to threatening situations differ widely from one person to another, but it's becoming more recognized that in addition to fight or flight, "freeze" is also common. Until we recognize this, our society will continue to treat rape victims with *perfectly normal* psychological traits as untrustworthy.

Schumer effectively ridicules the idea that the victim's choices have anything to do with the incidence of rape in America, by leaving those choices completely out of the picture. In a sketch called "Everyone for Themselves!," Schumer's character attends a prenatal yoga class, where she and the other expectant mothers share worries their child might grow up to enjoy SantaCon, commit rape, or "do something unforgiveable," like (gasp!) become a DJ.

Like the football sketch, the listing of rape alongside quirky but benign preferences highlights the normalization of rape in mainstream society, and it reduces to absurdity the idea that rape is natural and inevitable. The sketch also illustrates the moral irrelevance of the *victim's* choices and actions, by placing the responsibility squarely on the rapist, and those who would reduce a fundamental violation of human rights to a mere "quirky fetish." The victim's subjective response to rape is—surprise!—completely beside the point.

The "Barbarian Rapist"

Some rapists go free or receive special treatment because they do not fit the stereotype of the "barbarian rapist"—poor, uneducated, and racialized. To give a well-known example, Brock Turner, a white Stanford University student and varsity athlete, received only six months' jail time for raping an unconscious woman after a party. He was caught red-handed by two other students. Turner's status as an affluent, athletic, educated male, along with his visible (white) racial attributes were thought to have influenced the judge's decision, and this sparked international protests. Since Turner's sentencing, these protests have prompted California lawmakers to introduce minimum mandatory sentences for rape (which minimized the role of the perpetrator's socio-economic status and racialized attributes in judicial sentencing).

The myth of the racialized perpetrator exists because African-American men are stereotyped as sexual predators in our culture. Critical race theorist Tommy Curry points out that the cultural schema of "Black Maleness" involves two contradictory stereotypes: Black men are seen as aggressive sexual predators on the one hand, and as childish and intellectually immature on the other. This creates the absurd stereotype of the Child Rapist, which deprives Black men of any coherent identity in our shared cultural space. More to the point for us, the bogeyman of the "Black male rapist" helps to explain why white rapists get comparatively lenient sentences. While Turner got only six months in jail, a Black man named Brian Banks served five years in prison for a sex crime that he didn't commit.

Recognizing the white men are no less likely than Black men to commit rape will help to correct the racial bias that beleaguers the US justice system, and will also help women prosecute the majority of rapists in America: white males. (According to *Sex Offenses and Offenders*, nearly 99 percent of sex offenders in single-victim incidents were male and *60 percent were white.)* Thus, rejecting the stereotype of the Black Male Rapist will help to reduce two biases that protect white rapists: racism and sexism.

Schumer's comedy does occasionally touch on racial injustice. In a sketch called "Generations," Schumer's character brings home a Hispanic boyfriend for dinner, and, to her mortification, her family mistakes him for a server and hands him their dirty dishes to be washed. The sketch then cuts to a commercial for "Generations," a rehabilitation program for people "suffering from" acculturated racism. The clients are trained to suppress their racial biases by, for example, not calling for the lifeguard when a Black man jumps into a swimming pool, and not clutching their purse at the sight of a cardboard cut-out of a Black man. This last scene uses humour to bring into relief the insidious criminalization of Black men described by Tommy Curry, which helps to explain why white defendants receive lighter sentences than Black defendants across all crimes, including sexual assault. In other words, Schumer uses humour to illuminate a serious flaw in the justice system.

The Damsel in Distress

Schumer devotes a chapter of her autobiography to her lived experience as a survivor of rape and intimate partner violence. She uses personal narratives to debunk the myth that rape victims are weak, indecisive, and "damsels in distress," as opposed to "strong-ass women." This damsel-in-distress stereotype once again hearkens back to coverture law, which entails that married women cannot speak for themselves. Accordingly, outspoken women were seen as unlikable, untrustworthy, and seditious—and to some extent, they still are. This is why, even in modern times, "real rape victims" are stereotyped as quiet, submissive, and dependent, while gender non-conforming women who are independent, assertive, and opinionated, are seen as unrapeable: that is, their testimony tends to be seen as less credible.

The situation faced by the modern woman is described by prominent feminists like Talia Mae Bettcher as a "double bind," in which stereotypically feminine women are well-liked but dismissed, while stereotypically masculine (non-conforming) women are generally disliked but taken more seriously. This gives rise to a damned if you do, damned if you don't dilemma, where there are costs to both options—costs that men never have to pay.

Sadly, non-stereotypical rape victims are even more damned than non-stereotypical women in general, as they are both *disliked and discredited.* In a 2005 survey, subjects rated rape allegations from a same-sex female partner as more believable when one partner was butch and the other was femme. This suggests that people have difficulty imagining that rape could be perpetrated on a masculine woman. Hence, women with stereotypically masculine features who report rape may be seen as less credible.

Schumer attacks this stereotype by revealing that she—a self-professed strong-ass woman—has been raped in unequivocal terms. Her traits of independence, confidence, and assertiveness do not insulate her from sexual violence, no matter what society presumes about her. The fact that this might come as a shock to some readers shows how susceptible we are to the stereotype of the "feminine rape victim." Schumer's personal narrative drives home that rape victims are not a specific type of person: they are every type of person.

Schumer also attacks a second, related stereotype in her book: that strong-ass women cannot be victims of intimate partner violence. In *The Girl with the Lower Back Tattoo*, she relates her experience of living with an abusive partner for over a year, and asserts that intimate partner violence "can happen to anyone" (p. 300).

Schumer is right that anyone can find herself in a situation of domestic abuse. But there is a huge caveat here: just because you *can* be trapped in an abusive relationship, it doesn't follow that you must be. Unlike laboratory animals, which develop learned helplessness in response to pain and cannot escape painful conditions when given the chance, human beings have free will and can exercise it to choose amongst a range of options.

The characteristic features of an abusive relationship, as defined by the Center for Disease Control, are: 1. physical violence; 2. sexual violence, including rape and unwanted sexual contact; 3. stalking or repeated, unwanted attention and contact; and 4. psychological aggression, including name-calling, humiliation, limiting access to transportation, money or social contacts, excessive monitoring, threats, presenting false information, and "mind games." By being mindful of these conditions, we can better protect ourselves and other women against intimate partner violence.

Another critical factor is access to safe and affordable housing, legal resources, counseling, and decent wages, which are not equally available to everyone. (Women are particularly vulnerable to intimate partner violence, as well as low wages). While women's safe houses provide resources to women and their children, they are forced to turn away thousands of applicants every year due to insufficient funds. Perhaps if governments and policy-makers better understood the scope and impact of sexual violence, they would invest more in resources for victims of intimate partner violence.

Schumer is contributing to the cultural conversation about these issues and nudging society in the right direction.

The Moral of the Story

Not all of the stereotypes described here are mutually consistent, but this does not mean that they don't exist. We can and do hold inconsistent implicit attitudes at the same time. Thus, we can discriminate against both stereotypically heterosexual wives and non-gender-conforming single women at the same time on an unconscious level. This explains how double binds are possible, which provoke discrimination against opposite groups at the same time.

Does the existence of grape zones imply that people are not responsible for acting on implicit rape-positive attitudes? Not at all. As we saw, not all people hold implicit biases to the same extent, and we can modify these biases using cognitive strategies and exposure to counter-stereotypical images (such as Schumer's stand-up persona). The football players in "Football Town Nights" *are* responsible for their behavior, and they *can* be prosecuted in a court of law. We all have a standing responsibility to acquaint ourselves with the law and abide by it (with the exception of people who are psychotic and qualify for involuntary hospitalization under the insanity defence). But in the vast majority of cases, people who break the law are legally liable.

In addition to our civic duty to abide by the law, we have a standing *moral* duty to reject harmful biases that reinforce patriarchal relations and create a culture of gendered sexual violence. If we fail to do this, we are morally blameworthy. Hence, as citizens and moral agents, we have a legal and moral responsibility to think critically about grape zones and reject the false stereotypes that make them possible.

Schumer's brand of comedy is helping to do this. By ridiculing the rapist's perspective, comedians increase public knowledge about rape and lend credibility to the victim's standpoint. This is a major feat for feminism and a massive blow to rape culture.

15
Are There Certain Things We Should Not Talk About?

VERENA EHRNBERGER

> Enough ink has flowed over the quarrel about feminism; it is now almost over: let's not talk about it any more.
>
> —SIMONE DE BEAUVOIR, 1949

Yet here we are, still talking about "female" comics, as if comedy were inherently male. In her book, *The Girl with the Lower Back Tattoo,* Amy Schumer responds to the phenomenon of "female comedy" in her typical power-of-the-truth type of way:

> First, I'd like to thank all the people who pointed out that I was a woman. Your compliments were phrased very precisely so that I was never just described as "funny," but rather, as a "funny woman." You made sure I didn't lose sight of my ovaries. Thank you. (pp. 270–71)

As a comedian, Amy talks about what all girls talk about: Sexting. One night stands. Porn. Beauty standards. Slut Shaming. As we all know, there's hardly anything girls do *not* talk about. The only difference with Amy Schumer is that she does it publicly.

Existentialist philosopher Simone de Beauvoir also dared to speak out about female issues publicly. Like today, there were certain things you should not openly talk about. (In Simone de Beauvoir's time, this was mostly women's menstruation. Then again, in our times, it still is . . .).

Simone de Beauvoir dedicated her often discussed book, *The Second Sex,* to things that should not be talked about when it comes to women. She argues that man sees woman as "the Other": he doesn't define her in herself, but in relation to himself—essentially not asking "What is she?" but "What is she to me?" Being "the Other," women are surrounded by an aura of mystery. Through this mystification, women are made into creatures that cannot be understood. And society would rather it stayed that way.

Talking publicly about women's issues, like Amy Schumer does, is still a pretty bold thing to do—even in our times. It is not considered normal (as one might think, in a modern society). It is considered feminist.

Making Feminism Fun Again

> One of the benefits that oppression secures for the oppressor is that the humblest among them feels superior.
>
> —Simone de Beauvoir

When Amy states, "I'm Amy Schumer, and I'm proud to say that I'm a feminist," in her sketch *Gang Bang*, before almost having sex with a parade of not very sexy average Joes, she is more right than the title of her sketch might suggest.

For most people, feminism has become something that somehow leaves a bitter taste. Hardly anyone makes a fuss about unequal pay, sexual harassment, or double standards. This is not because the times have changed; and it's not because gender inequality isn't still an issue. People have stopped talking about it because things *didn't* change. For a long time. It's just tiring to be upset about the status quo all the time.

In addition, feminism has been misunderstood and misused in the past decades. It has been used to counter men's macho attitudes, and even to shame women for not being feminist enough, according to some high (and therefore superior) feminist standards. This way, feminism—a movement which had liberation as its goal—has been turned into a tool of oppression. And that's just no fun at all. (Neither for men nor for women.)

Amy makes feminism fun again. Instead of pointing fingers, she is delivering harsh truths with a smile. By doing so, she shows us that the feminist discourse doesn't necessarily have to be led in a dead serious way. "We all accept too easily that life has to be hard and forget to make sure we have the most fun we can," Amy says in her book (p. 301). "I look at the saddest things in life and laugh at how awful they are, because they are hilarious and it's all we can do with moments that are painful" (p. 56). Every time we experience yet another example of gender inequality is one of these moments.

Instead of bashing men and focusing on male privilege and injustice, Amy (and many other feminists of her generation) make women the center of the discussion, by showing women as they really are. They thereby contribute, in a fun and approachable way, to the discussion about gender equality, that we, as a society, still need to have. (Especially, when today's understanding of feminism might include hosting a gang bang to demonstrate that women are not objects.)

Just so we are clear: Feminism is not about being better than men, about toughening up in a man's world or beating men with their own weapons. Women who obey masculine power logics (or even use them to get ahead of other women) have not understood that feminism has nothing to do with oppressing the oppressor in some vain attempt at revenge (or objectifying the objectifier, like Amy fails to do in "Gang Bang").

A feminist attitude is an attitude that fosters equality and mutual respect. A feminist attitude has nothing to do with being a woman, and everything to do with being a human being. This kind of feminist attitude—adopted by women and men alike—is still necessary to challenge the status quo we oftentimes mistake for the natural order of things.

In sketch after sketch, Amy points out the absurdity of the status quo, and reminds us that it was developed by men in an attempt to define women. Feminism is about getting the chance to define ourselves, without somebody doing it for us. Feminism has nothing to do with oppression or counter-oppression, but rather a lot to do with contemplating what constitutes a woman. Feminism is about being a human being, equal to all other human beings, and respectful towards all of them. And, last but not least, it is about having the courage to call bullshit on any type of oppression. Amy demonstrates this kind of attitude every time she gets on stage.

What Constitutes a Woman?

> We are told that "femininity is in jeopardy"; we are urged, "Be women, stay women, become women."
>
> —Simone de Beauvoir

"Femininity" is still something that is mysterious as well as misunderstood. What is a woman? Our take on femininity is very much influenced by what we see, especially in the media. Think about how women look in the movies, on billboards, on television. And then think about who probably made the decision to design them that way.

In her sketch, "12 Angry Men Inside Amy Schumer," Amy challenges our current portrayal of "femininity" in the media. Twelve men of the jury discuss one central question: Is Amy Schumer hot enough to be on television?

"It's an undisputed fact that a woman's value is mostly determined by her looks," one of the men says. They start arguing about whether Amy is bangable or not, and whether she belongs to categories like "protagonist hot," "whacky neighbor," or "divorced obese woman with a funny dog." They ponder the further consequences of their decision: "The point is, the more she's out there flaunting her chipmunk face, the more her type becomes acceptable." After a long discussion, the men agree that there might be circumstances under which they would, in fact, possibly bang her, and therefore conclude that they should allow her appearance on television.

In another sketch, "Plain Jane," Amy plays an undercover cop who is particularly successful in her job, because she is so unattractive that she's invisible. Her chief acknowledges her accomplishments by exclaiming "God dammit, plain Jane, if only inner beauty mattered!" In "I'm So Bad," women add the obligatory phrase "I'm so bad!" whenever one of them admits to eating something that could ruin their perfect figure, while they keep reassuring each other that they still look skinny. These sketches reflect the image society has destined for women: Be beautiful, stay skinny, become a mystery.

Simone de Beauvoir pointed out in *The Second Sex* what this understanding of womanhood really means: "Not every female human being is necessarily a woman; she must take part in this mysterious and endangered reality known as femininity." But this reality of femininity that women are expected to comply with, and that determines the way women should look and behave, is based on male decisions. (It may even be based on the decision of twelve angry men stuck together in a room.) Women adopt this so-called "standard" of femininity without questioning it, and without even being part of the discussion. (A discussion that might take place in a room in which women are not allowed.)

A "real woman," as it seems, is a mysterious and marvelous being. She dresses up, puts on make-up and transforms herself into a goddess. Simone de Beauvoir understood the function of this dressing-up as a way to complete "woman's metamorphosis into an idol." A "real woman" is aware of the role she has to play in a male world. She has to be beautiful, skinny, and sexy. Her job is, basically, to represent sex. In her sketch "Sex Prep," Amy shows all the steps women have to take to become this perfect goddess-like creature that men feel comfortable banging. This metamorphosis includes not eating, cutting your nails, dying your hair, getting rid of all your body hair, being available whenever he wants it (even if that means quitting your job), refurbishing your face with make-up, putting on a sexy dress and an enjoyable attitude, giving yourself some liquid courage (or maybe that's just Amy), cleaning up your apartment to create a nice environment, finding the most sexy position to sit in on your couch and faking interest. In the end of this sketch, Amy can't take the pressure of all this feminine perfection and hides under her bed. (Because that's what a real woman does!) The sketch concludes with the phrase, "Amy never had sex again."

Perfection can be tempting. It can soothe our vulnerable human egos to be considered a mysterious and perfect being. But if women are mystified to be that perfect human being, the conclusion might be that women are only allowed to be just that. The problem with perfection is that it ultimately leads to self-suppression—and maybe even to adding the phrase "I'm so bad!" whenever we do something that could ruin that perfect image. "We will not let ourselves be fooled by the self-serving praise showered on the 'real woman'," Simone de Beauvoir wrote. Or have we?

Amy certainly has not: "So I guess, like, some guys, they wanna sleep with a girl that's, like, a skeleton wrapped in plastic. That's fine if that's what you want. But I'm gonna keep eating, and showering infrequently" (*Inside Amy Schumer*, "Meth Lab").

The Mysterious Concept of Womanhood

> Man in all societies is protected against the feminine sex's threats by so many taboos.
>
> —Simone de Beauvoir

"Are you that girl from the television that talks about her pussy all the time?" Julia Louise-Dreyfus (Elaine from *Seinfeld*) asks, when Amy stumbles upon some of her show-business heroines in her sketch, "Last Fuckable Day."

At first sight, it might seem like Amy Schumer just talks about all those annoying things women in the twenty-first century are frequently confronted with and can therefore easily relate to: the ridiculousness of online dating, the distortion of real intimacy by porn, and the general objectification of women by society. And, of course, she raises one of the most important questions of our century: What's the best possible angle for a naked selfie? But that's all on the surface. What Amy really talks about a lot (besides her pussy) is gender inequality.

One truly remarkable thing about Amy Schumer is her ability to address inequality issues that feel so natural to us that we hardly question them anymore. "Last Fuckable Day" is about the fact that women's sexuality has an expiration date. While men presumably get better with age (or at least, that's what we're led to believe), women, who dress up as perfect sexy idols all their life, suddenly stop being "real women" when they cannot compete with younger women, who are just getting started dressing up as perfect sexy idols all their life. When we watch this sketch, we can't help but notice two things. First of all: This is so true! And second: What the hell is up with that? Of course, in this sketch, the Last Fuckable Day is something worth celebrating. Because, let's be honest: Who wants to dress up as a perfect sexy idol for the rest of their life?

According to Simone de Beauvoir, man invented woman as a mysterious creature that is "everything he craves and everything he does not attain." Psychologically speaking, man needs "the Other" to experience himself: "He projects onto her what he desires and fears, what he loves and what he hates." To fulfill this role that man subconsciously intended for her, woman has to be a mystery. Of course, being a mystery has many other advantages too. "It allows an easy explanation for anything that is inexplicable," Simone de Beauvoir argues. This way, man doesn't have to understand female realities (like menstruation or childbirth), because the mysteries of femininity are simply too difficult to grasp. Mystery can serve as an excuse.

And what better way to preserve a mystery than by further veiling it with a taboo? It is the mysterious things, we do not talk about. By keeping quiet about certain female issues, the mystery of "the Other" stays intact. Taboos serve to cover up truths that are somehow unsettling—like, for men, the fact that their perfect, mysterious, idol-like women can age. By making them the mysterious Other, men have put women on a pedestal, and they would rather keep them there. So, when women age, they are not considered "real women" anymore (aka the Last Fuckable Day), and start being considered an asexual being. All of this makes perfect sense, if you follow the logic that a woman represents sex, and sex only. The aging woman therefore has to be covered up by a taboo.

When it comes to women, there are many things we, as a society, do not really talk about: menstruation, childbirth, marital sexual desire—basically everything that makes a woman seem like an actual human being instead of a mystical creature bordering on perfection. This is especially true for all of her bodily functions. The fact that women use the toilet like men, burp, barf and fart like men, is unmentionable, even today. If you stop to think about it, you can't help but realize that all those taboos surrounding women coincide with things that threaten the image of woman as the representation of sex.

The taboos surrounding women have stayed more or less the same since the times of Simone de Beauvoir, who wrote *The Second Sex* in 1949. Thankfully, there are also some taboos that we seem to have been able to shake. Today, for example, it's okay for women to have sexual desires. They are even expected to. (Sexual desire goes very well with woman's job as the representation of sex, after all.) But female sexual desire in a marriage is oftentimes still considered a taboo. That's what we see in "Sex Stories." In this sketch, Amy's husband (played by Zach Braff) gets silenced by his friends at the poker table any time he wants to join into their conversation about sex stories, because he is not talking about some anonymous girl, but about his wife. The wife's role is something other than the role the "real woman" has to play. The wife has to be nurturing and domestic. Talking about her as a sexual being is the taboo here.

"Isn't it funny that they say most girls have daddy issues, when really, every dude does?" Amy writes. (p. 85) The observation she is making here is that having issues isn't the birthright of a specific sex. There is no real difference between the issues men and women have to face. The biggest myth of them all is the concept of womanhood itself, as Simone de Beauvoir points out.

It is, without a doubt, a fact of the biological sciences that there are two different sexes. But there is no factual evidence that women and men necessarily have to behave in different ways. Still, we attribute certain gender roles to the biological sexes. Gender roles are socially constructed roles that have nothing to do with the biological sex. Today, we all know that. Still, we somehow expect men and women to behave according to their gender roles. In other words, women get to have daddy issues while men don't.

"Women get a reputation for being the crazy, overly sensitive ones in relationships, but in my experience, it's the dudes who do that," Amy says about the gender portrayal in her movie *Trainwreck*. When we see men or women not acting in alignment with their gender role (that society sometime in the past arbitrarily made up for them), we experience this behavior as "gender role reversal" (see "Switching It Up," in this book), and not simply as human nature.

Keeping It Real

> The more women assert themselves as human beings, the more the marvelous quality of Other dies in them.
>
> —Simone de Beauvoir

Amy Schumer asserts herself as a flawed fuckup. "I don't even want to know someone who isn't barely hanging on by a thread," she writes (p. 20). The initial question of this chapter—are there certain things we should not talk about?—could also be phrased like this: "Why do you think it's okay to make people uncomfortable?" This is a question Amy

Schumer actually got asked during an interview. And it sums up why her comedy is considered controversial.

We're used to taboos. We're used to not talking about certain things that make us feel uncomfortable. Some people need the comfort of taboos. And Amy is obviously all about breaking them, because she knows that taboos silence people from speaking up about things that are important to speak up about.

Amy leaves very little of womanhood to mystery, and thereby restores power. Because things tend to get pretty powerful once we talk about them. Demystification is all about being real. But being a real human being can be terrifying. It means admitting to flaws. In her book, Amy describes a humiliating childhood memory and concludes: "This was my very first experience of the stripped-down, cold, unprotected space where vulnerability meets either confidence or shame. It was my choice, and I had to learn (I'm still learning) how to choose to be proud of who I am rather than ashamed" (pp. 312–13). Vulnerability can be pretty powerful. It is the prerequisite for being real.

Amy decided not to be ashamed of her flaws, but to own them by laughing about them, rather than concealing them. Amy's jokes celebrate vulnerability, and they show that there isn't really anything to be ashamed of. Jokes can be empowering. "Life is full of pain and disappointment. I've made a whole career out of pointing this out and reliving it in ridiculous ways so everyone can laugh and cry along with me" (p. 237). Amy makes us laugh about fundamentally unjust circumstances. By laughing about it, it no longer has so much power over us. By laughing about it, we simply decide not to take these kinds of things seriously. This is what's so powerful about asserting oneself as a flawed fuckup: "I wear my mistakes like badges of honor, and I celebrate them. They make me human" (p. 310).

In *The Girl With The Lower Back Tattoo,* Amy decided to publish some of her old journal entries: "Many people think I have this unshakable confidence, so I hope this look into my most intimate thoughts will support the idea that loving yourself takes time. Like any healthy relationship, it doesn't happen overnight" (pp. 130–31, footnote 15).

There are many people out there who prefer the truth over a pretty taboo. So, we all should follow Amy's example and keep telling it. As Simone de Beauvoir said, "Mystery is never more than a mirage; it vanishes as soon as one tries to approach it."

16
Raucous Feminist or Racially Insensitive?

JENNIFER WARE

Amy Schumer is deeply interested in women's issues. The back cover of Schumer's memoir, *The Girl with the Lower Back Tattoo*, describes Schumer as "one of the most sought-after comedians on the planet and an outspoken advocate for women's rights."

We don't have to dig too deep to confirm that both of these characterizations accurately describe Schumer and what she thinks and does, both on and off the stage. In her memoir, for example, Schumer dedicates multiple chapters to discussions of the unfair standards women regularly face regarding work, sex, and even just our appearances. She takes up issues of sexual assault and domestic violence in powerfully written chapters titled "How I Lost My Virginity" and "The Worst Night of My Life." She writes in a way that is intended to affirm and empower.

In her television series, *Inside Amy Schumer*, she addresses the superficial standards placed on women in entertainment ("You Would Bang Her?," "Last Fuckable Day," "12 Angry Men Inside Amy Schumer"), along with jokes about how women are conditioned to apologize for themselves ("I'm Sorry"), and she even confronts rape culture ("A Very Realistic Military Game," "Football Town Nights").

Schumer won a Peabody award in 2014 for her "admirably feminist dedication to challenging and disrupting gendered expectations of women's behavior." Her "raucous feminist humor" is celebrated in a *New York Times* article discussing her show's increasingly political third season. At the same time, an article in *The Guardian* accuses Schumer of having a blind spot for race, and a writer for the *Daily Beast* described Schumer's feminism as "white-washed." An article on *Elite Daily* warns against turning Schumer into a feminism icon. So is Schumer a feminist or not? And if she is, is she a *good* one?

Feminism and Intersectionality

Often, feminism is talked about as if it's a single, well-defined position. People in the media will talk about feminists, or people will appeal to the idea of feminism to make this or that point. And when they refer to "feminism" like that, we assume there's something they mean by that word. However, there are many different sets of beliefs that can be identified as feminist, and many people who identify as feminists disagree with one another about what that means. One thing that is true for all feminists is that there is a need for social change. But then again, different feminists disagree, sometimes radically, about what *kinds* of changes are called for. Basically, feminism is a large, varied set of ideas. One of the reasons we may disagree about whether something or someone is feminist is if we have different ideas about what feminism *is*.

One prominent type of feminist theory is liberal feminism. Liberal feminists tend to focus on creating space for women within existing systems from which they have historically been excluded, so that women can make free choices about what they do and who they are. For example, it has been argued that women have been relegated to the domestic domain to raise children and tend homes, while men have dominated the public domain. Because the public domain is where a person can obtain economic and political power, this exclusion has meant women are unable to exercise such authority. The prescribed response, then, is to make it so that women have the opportunity to exert influence in both the private and public realms. This involves doing things like fighting for the right to vote, for the right to work, and to place women in powerful roles in the workplace and in the government.

Many figures from the liberal feminist world are likely to spring to mind when thinking about feminism more generally—Susan B. Anthony, for example. Anthony's contributions and the work done by other suffragettes to fight for (some) women's right to vote is an example of this way of approaching the imbalance of power between men and women. We might also think of famous liberal feminist Betty Friedan. In 1963, Friedan published *The Feminine Mystique*. In this book, she tries to articulate what she calls "the problem that has no name," an affliction she believes to be common among women at the time. She describes it as the feeling of emptiness and restlessness that comes from being confined to the home and denied the ability to work and pursue self-development in other ways.

Another type of feminism, which is often contrasted with liberal feminism, is a type of feminist theory called "intersectionality." Intersectionality is most notably distinguished by its focus on the complexity of identity. Intersectional feminists point out that many liberal feminists speak as if the world were divided into groups solely based along the lines of gender, so that each person is *most essentially* either a man or a woman. The gender category to which a person belongs is then treated as the most significant factor in whether or how that person is oppressed.

But in fact, the intersectional feminist points out, individuals are members of many groups, and their identities are shaped not only by gender but also by race, sexual orientation, class, cognitive or physical ability, and so on. Each of these dimensions or domains of identity shapes who a person is and how that person is situated in the power dynamics of society. To think otherwise is not a benign error, and so the liberal feminist is not only incorrect, but also contributing to further injustice.

Let's consider two prominent criticisms that intersectional feminists make of liberal feminists who neglect to consider the influences of these other identity constituents. First, there is the criticism that such liberal feminists speak as if what they are saying represents the experiences, needs, oppressions, and desires of all women—when, in fact, those experiences are quite restricted and typically apply mostly to white, middle-class women, women with relatively more resources and power. It's only because of their increased resources and power that liberal feminists are able to present themselves as if they are the face of women more generally. They can leverage their relative social position to gain access to the public stage. Many women with far different experiences, who may be oppressed in a multitude of ways (along a multitude of dimensions), lack access to that stage, and thus their experiences are silenced and further erased by the more visible presence of the relatively privileged women speaking "for" them.

In *Feminist Theory: From Margin to Center*, intersectional feminist bell hooks responded to Betty Friedan's claim that women suffer from a sort of existential crisis as a result of being confined to the home. She noted that many women of color have had no choice but to work. Thus, the problem is not a women's problem, but rather a problem for mostly white, middle-class, educated women. To confuse the two, or to claim that these problems apply to women in general, and not just a small subset of women, is to render non-white, non-middle class, non-educated women invisible.

The second problem leveled against liberal feminists by intersectional feminists, is that liberal feminists fail to recognize their own privileges. Intersectional feminists argue for the possibility of being oppressed along one dimension of identity while at the same time experiencing privilege along another. For example, a gay man may be oppressed in virtue of his homosexuality (if he lives in a society that systematically discriminates against that identity). At the same time, he may also be privileged in virtue of his being a man (if he lives in a society that systematically rewards that identity).

Liberal feminists are accused of failing to recognize that while they may be systematically disadvantaged in virtue of being women, they also benefit from an existing structure like white privilege. In virtue of their relative privilege, they have choices and can wield power that other women cannot.

Intersectional theorists and activists have argued that if women are obtaining power in virtue of oppressive systems like white privilege, then those gains will come at a cost for women who are oppressed in other ways. True change requires greater deconstruction than campaigns to produce more women CEOs.

Back to Schumer

Arguably, Amy Schumer's body of work may be criticized on two fronts. She has both represented herself as speaking for women generally while actually speaking only for and to women who look and live like her, *and* she has made jokes at the expense of women of color and appropriated work that is not hers to use.

In a series of jokes during her first full-length stand up special, *Mostly Sex Stuff,* Schumer comments on the kinds of difficulties women face. She repeatedly attributes these difficulties to women in an unqualified way, as if she is talking about women in the most general sense—all women. Most of the difficulties involve the superficial expectations women face to look great all the time, to wear heels and make-up and to spend hours "getting ready" (whereas men are permitted to spend far less time on their appearances). This reduction of hardships to the frivolous details of "getting ready" and Schumer's repeated references to dolled up women as "whores" may already be alarming, but during a discussion of the expectation that women groom or remove their pubic hair, she comments that the women who provide waxing services are never white women like her, but rather women "from a third world country."

She follows this story with a self-critical comment that "we're the worst, white entitled girls," but then tells another joke that suggests the women she is talking to are not, in fact, *all* the women in the audience, some of whom are not white girls. At the start of a series of jokes about race, Schumer says, "It doesn't matter what you do ladies, every guy is going to leave you for an Asian woman." This kind of joke, along with the line about bikini waxers, creates a division between women and *other* women. There's one group being labeled "women"—those who are really probably the white women that Schumer then bemoans—and the *other* women, who come in as the foils in each joke (third-world women, Asian women).

And then there's the Beyoncé controversy. In 2016, Schumer and her *Snatched* co-star Goldie Hawn lip-synced and danced to Beyoncé's *Formation* in a music video that came under instant fire by online commentators. The lyrics of *Formation* frequently refer to Beyoncé's identity as a black woman, and the original music video takes on the issue of police violence. In all, it is a work that directly confronts issues of identity and politics. For these reasons, many online commentators felt that the choices made by Schumer and Hawn to create a video of the song were disrespectful, appropriative, and racially insensitive.

The song and original video were, in an important sense, *not for* Schumer. While many people can enjoy music created by people who are very different from them, sometimes artists create music that they want particular audience members to identify with. Ultimately, Schumer's life and experiences are very different from the ones described by the character created throughout Beyoncé's *Formation* album. Even so, she felt she had the right to make use of it for her purposes. Schumer defended the video as being an empowering project put together by the women involved in the movie. But I think this defense in the name of women only highlights the problem. Schumer found her actions defensible, because she is a woman and she felt that she was doing something for women. However, her identity as a woman does not mean *all* work by women is *for* her. To assume that it would be is to neglect the important differences in the experiences of women based on their complex, intersectional identities.

Lighten Up?

Maybe this is all a bit too serious. Maybe the right thing to do is to lighten up.

This objection could mean that it is inappropriate to evaluate comedians in the way that has been suggested. After all, their jobs and presumably their intentions are to make us laugh. It is undeniable that inappropriate content often elicits laughter, so maybe we're making an important mistake when we evaluate someone like Schumer, or any other comedian for that matter, using political or social criteria of these kinds. She's not a politician, she's not an academic, so why are we judging her for being a bad politician and a bad academic? Maybe this is just all a big misunderstanding.

Responding to this kind of objection raises larger questions about the moral and political significance of comedy and the moral and political responsibilities of comedians, ones that we could neither answer here nor in a much longer piece or book. However, it does seem that if any comedians can or should be held accountable for the ideas they put into the world, then comedians who self-identify as political, as Schumer does, should be candidates for such evaluations. But there's something else that this request to *lighten up* might be getting at, and I think it is a potentially more promising defense of what Schumer does in her writing and her performances.

Maybe our feeling that at times Schumer's comedic persona is vapid and selfish is *exactly the point*. Perhaps we are supposed to balk at the idea that Schumer can or is speaking for women generally when she makes claims about the problems women face. After all, how could she? How could anyone? We are all restricted to our own experiences and perspectives.

Schumer does sometimes seem acutely aware of her identity as a sometimes disadvantaged but often privileged woman with many opportunities at her disposal. In the first episode of Season Two of *Inside Amy Schumer*, the character of God observes Schumer's vapid character—a persona she often embodies on screen and in her standup—and reflects that he "should stop making so many white girls." She also goes out of her way to recognize how fortunate she was as a child and how fortunate she now is as a result of her professional success in a memoir chapter titled "On Being New Money."

So maybe we should lighten up—but not because Schumer's just kidding and jokes don't matter. Jokes *do* matter, but Schumer is in on the joke. She *makes herself* the joke. In this sense, to lighten up isn't to dismiss the self-indulgence and self-pitying of Schumer the character, but rather to recognize that Schumer the person is winking at us from inside. We should recognize that Schumer herself finds this character troubling and often unbearable. While it may be a part of who she is, it is also probably a part of who many of her viewers are. And it's possible that this unsavoriness we see in her performance may spark genuine reflection for those viewers who may not like what they see, in her or in themselves.

When Schumer plays a woman in "Herpes Scare" who would rather God "kill off an entire village in Uzbekistan" than accept that she has herpes, we see a caricature of a clearly despicable and self-centered person. The absurdity of such an attitude and its indefensibility suggests that the Schumer on the screen is not speaking for herself (or, at least, not a version of herself she thinks is defensible). Rather, she is playing an exaggerated character that is there to make us laugh and cringe.

Schumer has defended herself along these lines, writing that during performances she goes "in and out of playing an irreverent idea. That includes making dumb jokes about race . . . Trust me. I am not racist. I am a devout feminist and lover of all people." While some aspects of Schumer's work might initially raise an eyebrow only to be followed by a wink, there are other things that are a bit harder to stomach.

When she suggests in *Mostly Sex Stuff* that delivery rooms should be equipped with Google search engines so that black mothers inclined to name their babies things like "Tamambo" will be led to "better" names like "Jennifer," it is less obvious that the joke is supposed to be on Schumer's character. Rather, black women become the butt of the joke. When she jokes that she wants a to date a black man, but not one who is named Derrick, wears nice shirts, and has a job, it's no longer obvious that she's pointing a finger at the absurdity of the racist stereotype. Instead, her desire to date a "brotha" seems more like a reassertion of one.

One Step at a Time?

But hey, you might think, at least she's doing something! Even if Schumer's performances are not without reproach, perhaps we should be forgiving, because she is taking on serious and important issues. She's politicizing her work in ways that are difficult and make her vulnerable to criticism, and in doing so she's taking risks that it might be easier to avoid. After all, maybe it's too much to expect anyone to take on everything at once. We have to choose our battles, and maybe imperfect gains that liberal feminists may support are, in the end, beneficial for everyone. While this may seem like a reasonable response, it is also not a new one. Liberal feminists have often defended activism that has been identified as focusing on the problems of white women by arguing that something is better than nothing, and that it is unrealistic to expect that we have everything at once. Unfortunately, this tends to leave the most vulnerable women at the back of the march.

Requiring people in oppressed positions to wait until their equality is *realistic* is troubling on its own, and intersectional theorists like Kimberlé Crenshaw have argued that focusing on a single dimension of oppression leaves out people who are "multiply-burdened." But we also have to note that Schumer has responded dismissively to charges that her work is insensitive. In response to the criticism she received for the *Forma-*

tion video, Schumer tweeted, "You know you that bitch when you cause all this conversation. Thank for the exclusive release Tidal! We had so much fun making this tribute. All love and women inspiring each other. #strongertogether."

Here again, Schumer defends her actions because they are motivated by feelings of unity with other women and with some intent to empower or inspire women generally. However, in doing so, she discharges the complaints of women who arguably have a more rightful claim to the material she appropriated and who feel her actions disregarded the differences between her experiences and theirs. When told she is not welcome, that she is not part of some particular conversation by and for women but women she cannot speak for, she dismissed the haters.

So Schumer has made some mistakes. Does that mean we should kick her out of the feminism club? Not at all. Does that mean that we're excusing her mistakes? Also no. It is possible to be a feminist and also imperfect.

Amy Schumer is a feminist and an imperfect one. She does feminist work with her comedy that is sometimes successful and sometimes problematic. We should not expect performers, even politically-minded and engaged ones like Schumer, never to misspeak or overstep. Art and performance require that boundaries are pushed and re-established, and social justice movements necessitate a willingness to transgress the status quo. However, we can expect that those performers take accountability for the things they say and do, especially when those actions violate their asserted values.

A raucous feminist with some racial insensitivities; Schumer can be and is both.

17
Switching It Up

GERALD BROWNING

The comedy of Amy Schumer draws on many themes, but one of the most prevalent of those themes is sex and intimacy. It's obvious that this particular theme is not an accident. A lot of Schumer's jokes seem to address the idea that we live in a male-dominated society. What better way to show this than by poking fun at the most sensitive of topics (to the male ego): sex?

The many double standards that we have with regard to gender roles and sex seem to embody the male viewpoint. One particular concept up for discussion is the *ownership* of sex (and, in particular, a woman's orgasm). We can address many quandaries about how sex can be seen as a male-dominated concept by looking at the idea of ownership. To make the ownership of sex a shared concept can be threatening to the male psyche (and the social structure as a whole).

To most of us, this may not seem like such a surprise; however, the concept of sex ownership highlights the absolute hypocrisy that stems from the social norms and attitudes about sex, as of now. In American society (as well as many others), sex (from a masculine perspective) is seen as an almost aggressive action. If a man's "conquests" are many, he's seen as a "player" or a "ladies' man" (or some other culturally-created noun phrase that subtly demeans women). Yet, when a woman acts in the same way, she is labeled a "slut" or a "whore" by society.

The idea extends not only to individuals but also to relations between individuals. When a woman is cheated on, she is stereotypically viewed as a naive or submissive woman who "should have known better"—after all, that's just how men act, right? (At least, that is, according to some stereotypes). Yet, when a man is cheated on, his masculinity is called into question—he must not have been man enough to take care of the needs of his wife. This hypocrisy is demonstrated in the Schumer hit *Trainwreck*. This movie tells the story of a woman who has the attitude that many young men seem to stereotypically have: sex should be something that has little to no emotional connection. Sex is nothing but fun, and commitment is something to be feared. An interesting point made in the movie is that this attitude towards intimacy is something that is systemic—something that we are taught early on and that we then assume in order to navigate the world.

In the film, there's a scene in which a young Schumer and her sister are given a lesson by their father (played by Colin Quinn) about how natural it is for someone to cheat on their spouse or significant other. Later on, we see how Schumer's character seems to have followed in her father's footsteps (jumping from one meaningless relationship to another). Schumer's sister, on the other hand, seems to have gotten into a marriage with a man whom she can boss around (thereby emasculating him). The stereotypes they've learned are enacted differently, but they are both a result of this early lesson.

The continued pattern of one-night stands (or shallow relationships) seems to come to an end when she meets a sports doctor about whom she is writing an article. They fall in love, and the doctor (played by Bill Hader) seems to realize it well before Schumer's character does. An article that turns into a one-night stand evolves (quite slowly, it seems) into a relationship. The character dynamic between Hader's character (Dr. Aaron Conners) and Schumer's character (Amy Townsend) seems to be the stereotypical commitment-phobe clashing with the ideals of their future-oriented partner. The twist is that the genders are reversed.

This gender reversal is perpetuated throughout the entire film, which ends when Amy makes a grand romantic gesture to win over the man she's realized she can't live without. Schumer (who does double duty as star and writer) pulls it off with charm.

Sports and (E)Masculinity

In Schumer's television series, as well as *Trainwreck*, she expresses little knowledge of sports; or rather, she makes a joke of how little she knows about sports. As she says in *Trainwreck*, "I just think that sports are stupid, and anyone who likes them is just, like, a lesser person. And has a small intellect." Schumer does a wonderful job using sports to pick at stereotypical notions of masculinity. In *Trainwreck*, she uses sports as the major backdrop to the story. Her love interest is a sports doctor that she has to interview. The joke of her ineptitude with athletics is an ongoing gag throughout the film. Athletes appear in several supporting roles, such as basketball player Lebron James (whether you love him or hate him, you have to admit that his role in the film is hilarious), John Cena (again, funny in his role), Tony Romo, Amar'e Stoudemire, Marv Albert, and Chris Evert.

One point worth mentioning here is the performances of two of these athletes: Lebron James and professional wrestler John Cena. These two are two of the major characters in the movie, and Schumer writes them in such a way as to point out how we not only stereotype men and their interest in sports, but the athletes themselves. The roles that these men play are quite similar to the roles women would play in a more "traditional" romantic comedy. Lebron James plays a character very different from who he is in reality. James, who is a best friend of Bill Hader's character, Aaron Conners, is overprotective of his friend. He expresses his concern for his friend, not in an uber-masculine way, but in a nosy, gossipy kind of way (note how these are adjectives typically applied to how women socialize). He constantly interrogates Aaron about Amy, and he gives Amy the third degree when they are sitting courtside at a charity game. (He assumes that his male doctor friend needs protection from his new girlfriend.) When interviewed after a game, the "real" Lebron James seems confident, but the Lebron that we see in the movie is endearingly awkward.

WWE professional wrestler John Cena is no stranger to acting. He plays Amy's boyfriend (at the beginning of the film), Steven. Even though Amy has no intentions of having a long-term relationship with him, he sees a future with Amy. In the traditional romantic comedy, we see a woman being head over heels in love with the leading male. In this movie, there is a reversal. Steven is devoted and committed to Amy, and he is oblivious to how she cheats on him. Once again, we have a professional athlete who is perceived as an opposite to the character that he portrays on the screen. This juxtaposition serves a way to satirize the masculinity that we project onto athletes.

The humor at Cena's expense pokes fun at masculinity itself. His character seems to be quite focused on his relationship with Amy (as well as personal fitness). Sometimes he combines those interests, as in the awkward dirty talking scene. He maps out his plan for his career, and it revolves around fitness and having lots of children with Schumer's character, who instantly shows her disdain. Continuing the humor at the expense of the gender disparity, the film shows how Cena's character is inept at teasing and threatening others. In a scene at the beginning of the film, a moviegoer is angry about how Amy is talking through a movie. To stand up for his girlfriend, Steven threatens the moviegoer. Unfortunately, his attempts to be threatening come off as pickup lines. "I will fuck you!" he says. He adds, "I will enter you!"

Owning the Orgasm

Schumer's standup routines often mention sex and the orgasm (which, as she points out, are two very different things). Some stereotypes are already at work: men initiate sex; it is the man who "gives" the woman the orgasm (while

Amy just lies there); a woman does not or cannot take control of her own enjoyment in the bedroom.

"Property" is usually defined as something to which someone has access or control over. In a patriarchal society, many people (specifically, the men-folk) are threatened by a woman who views sex (and achieving orgasm) as "hers" (her own property, as opposed to something bestowed upon her by a patriarch). In our world, men regularly make claims like, "I gave her an orgasm," as if an orgasm is something you can hand over to someone else (pun intended). The so-called masculine man is threatened by a woman who states, "I *gave* myself an orgasm"; this man owns the orgasms, and she must have stolen them from him. If only she were to say instead, "I *achieved* an orgasm." This latter statement creates a neutral voice. In other words, it can be perceived "openly" (no pun intended) as to who is responsible for the climax. In contrast, the use of the term "gave" attributes power (or *access*) firmly to the woman.

Another point that needs to be made here is the notion of competition within a patriarchal society. There is a constant battle of who is responsible for the orgasm which, as above, is easily phrased as an achievement. Sex isn't something that is seen as a mutually beneficial act, but as a competition. We compete to see who can rack up the most numbers or who can get to satisfactory completion sooner. Amy Schumer isn't the first (or the last) female comic who has joked about this very subject. During Schumer's HBO special, she quips "I'm very old school, I think the guy should always pay on the first date . . . for sex." The juxtaposition of the "old fashioned" notion of the man paying for the first date with sexual politics makes the joke that much more effective. (Note: There has been controversy surrounding this joke. Comedienne Wendy Liebman used a joke very similar to this well before the HBO special.)

So is Amy Schumer a "sex comic" or an "issue comic"? When a male comic makes jokes about sex, he is not labeled as a "sex comic" (he's a thinker, as Amy says); however, on many occasions, Schumer's sexual humor is used as an excuse to foist labels upon her. We begin to see how the politics of sex come into play. Labeling Schumer as a "sex comic" seems to pigeonhole her into a category that seems to be more comfortable for society, even though the way in which she jokes about sex relies more on identifying sexual stereotypes and calling them into question than it does on plain old sex jokes. It seems to me that we're more comfortable, as a society, to compartmentalize women who speak about sex as being "sex comics", as if to imply that "female comics" or "comediennes" are comics who do not speak about such things. (It would be unladylike.) Schumer does not strike me as a "sex comic". She strikes me as a comic who discusses real issues, and she sees sex as a real issue. That's why sex is a main punchline in much of her humor.

Don't Be a Such a Kant!

Immanuel Kant believed that sexuality is itself just a terrible thing. Sexuality can undermine one's values, and it makes the object of sexual desire an *object*, as opposed to another subject worthy of our respect. Many of Kant's references to sexual appetite have been viewed negatively for these reasons. Kant's view of sex is that it should be used purely for procreation and never for enjoyment; he believes that desiring someone sexually means that once the sexual desire is fulfilled, that person is tossed aside, "as one throws away a lemon after sucking the juice from it."

When we look at the patriarchal perspective and attitudes about sex, there is quite an overlap with Kant's theories. In this society, women can be objectified and reduced to a number. "How many women have you slept with?" This has been the subject of many jokes in Schumer's act. Many comediennes have addressed this theme. How many encounters does one have to have to be considered a "slut"? To count the number of lovers or encounters acts to objectify the partners that one has had—after all, if people weren't interchangeable objects, we wouldn't be able to add them up in our sexual tallies. Kant's theory is all about avoiding objectification, but it's not clear us now that the answer to avoiding objectification is to avoid sex all together, as he would have us do.

Kant believed that the most moral life is the life that is lived with sexual celibacy. He believed that sex corrupted people. It is no mystery as to why Kant saw sex in the way that he did. A proof of Kant's thesis is to observe the way in which sex stereotypically corrupts *men*. I would think that Schumer would agree with this notion. The astute reader of Kant would point out that women are not men, and that this concept of how sex works is dubitable when applied to the other gender. An even more astute reader might point out how pessimistic Kant's theory is about how men navigate sex.

Both in her movie and in her show, Schumer's humor seems to point out the fact that men are really not much different from women when it comes to sexual desire. In fact, she's very eager to point out similarities—the fact that women are similarly flawed when it comes to sexual matters. This brings up an important notion of "equality" in sexual politics. The equality of the sexes should allow for women to have the same *failings* that men have. To counter these failings, however, I do not believe we have to resort to Kant's solution. Despite recognizing human failings with regard to sex, Schumer would not agree with the idea that the most ethical life is the life with an absence of sex. That is to say, it seems obvious that Schumer does not necessarily look at celibacy as a way to a "moral" life.

The whole notion of "misogyny" depends on our seeing women as sexual objects and thus embodying Kant's theory. Meanwhile, comics such as Schumer make jokes about this, as a way to rail against this oppressive concept. (After all, it's hard to see how an object could make such hilarious observations about contemporary society.) In addition, by being able to "own" their orgasms and (in a way) sex itself, they are able to balance the equation, as it were. Along the way, we learn that sex isn't necessarily a negative notion (as Kant may surmise).

The comedy of Amy Schumer engages the audience and causes them to think (and re-evaluate) the relationships between men and women. We still do have the concept that "men are from Mars and women are from Venus", even though it now seems outdated and obsolete. But what does difference between people really do to the dynamics of equality and fairness? When the shoe is on the other foot, and we see a reversal in roles, as in *Trainwreck*, it seems easier to laugh at the social stigmas that abound. However, the reality is much less comical.

Schumer's comedy doesn't rely on the clichéd idea that women and men are fundamentally different sorts of beings. The woman isn't the one who always bails her man out and does the right thing (like in many sitcoms), and the man isn't always the commitment-phobe racking up one-night stands. She shows that what women do can exacerbate the idiocy of the patriarchal society that we live in. Sometimes, in her acting and in her sketch comedy, the biggest joke in Schumer's act is...Schumer herself. On many occasions, she refers to herself as a "whore" or "slut," but she doesn't do it in a way that unconsciously reinforces cultural stereotypes. She's completely self-aware. Even though these very diminutive and demeaning terms, in and of themselves, are degrading, she uses them to make a point, just as she does referring to men as "assholes" or "dicks."

And, just like men, women can actually enjoy sex. Just like men, women can be in control of the sex that they have with others. This ultimate power shift shows that Schumer's work is quite conscious of the disparity between men and women and seeks to ultimately right the scales (as it were). This seems to be where the "edginess" of Schumer's shtick seems to originate. Sex is looked at as a conquest and competition for many (especially males). However, when the notion of women enjoying sex and "owning" their own sexuality enters the equation, it appears that sex (and the act of it) becomes less of a competition and more about mutual gratification, which effectively takes away the competitive aspect of it.

At first glance, Amy Schumer may seem like your "run of the mill" sex comic. Her jokes are as raunchy as any male comic's. However, her humor goes well beyond poking fun at the foibles of male-female sexual encounters. One of the intriguing aspects of Schumer's standup is how perceptions are considered in relation to reality. When the discussion of "ownership" and sex is brought up, in a patriarchal society, sex can be seen as a war (or at least some sort of competitive sport, at which she'll also poke fun). Schumer's so-called sex comedy alludes to the discrepancies and double standards that the American society places upon its citizenry.

Schumer does not poke fun at sex, nor does she make the punchline about sex. Every joke seems to land just because her humor goes beyond mere sex. To lump Amy Schumer into the category of the "sex comic" is a mistake. Her punchlines do not merely deliver payload after payload. They go much deeper into the ideas of equality and an effective investigation (a scathing portrayal) of gender. She points out to us how some of our most absurd perceptions are shaped and, in turn, shaped by us.

Amy Schumer's humor readily addresses the idiosyncrasies that are apparent between the sexes. Interestingly enough, she shows these differences by pointing out the similarities between the genders. When we try to cope with the social perceptions of sex, the theme of "ownership" of sex is a great way to illuminate this notion. When identifying who is "responsible" for the satisfaction (or orgasm) of the participants, men and women are supposed to take different approaches to it. Yet, when a woman decides to take the ownership of her own satisfaction, it can affect the male's perception of his own masculinity.

These notions make the comedy of Amy Schumer so much more than sex comedy. Sure, Schumer makes many jokes about sex, but that does not necessarily make her a "sex comic." There is a deeper message in her jokes. There are more ideas that she needs to develop, so that people can see the genius and feminism in her work.

In many female comics' acts, there are kernels of empowerment. With Amy Schumer, the entire act is a message of empowerment.

V

Afterthoughts

18
Oppression Pretty Much Sucks

CHARLENE ELSBY AND ROB LUZECKY

The concept for *I Feel Pretty* is fucking awesome. How funny is it that a movie star, of all people, should be made to feel pretty? She must have some kind of head injury.

Sure, we know that movie stars are all supposed to be pretty, but we also think that they should be modest, because being modest is also pretty, and being conceited is ugly. So if someone who's pretty actually thinks they're pretty, they're right, but they're not pretty, so they're wrong. We just want them to be pretty but not *feel* pretty. Right? That's why it's so funny that Amy Schumer should think she's pretty. Or maybe she's been pretty all along, but she just didn't know it, and that makes her even prettier. Is that it?

Or is Amy Schumer brave? She did have the balls to do that nude photo shoot with Annie Leibovitz, which we think really shows how brave she is, admitting to having a human body while the rest of us run around covered in shame fabric. And by human, we don't mean to say, "She's just like the rest of us!" No. That was just after they made her lose all of that weight so that she could be a believable movie star in *Trainwreck*.

Sometimes we try to say things like, "Oh, she's so human," when what we mean to say is that she's as shitty of a human as I am. But that picture was hot, so that can't be it. How brave she was, though, not to cover up her hot body with various fabric flaps (clothing) that we all know serve a very important purpose: to introduce some mystery over the top of every living human's disgusting, revolting flesh form, the same flesh form, which probably would cause every other disgusting living human to recoil at any mere glimpse of it only to vomit in the corner for days (which also isn't pretty). Amy Schumer took that picture and showed us all that she doesn't have gills, a massive patch of thigh hair that she French braids, or even a conjoined twin who died in the womb but still lives on as her right knee. She has a human body—so brave.

Is it okay for a woman to say that Amy Schumer is hot? Women tend to all be socialized in the same way—to believe that we're garbage and that we should think we're garbage, and that every other living woman is a threat to one's own existence and that the only way to resolve this existential problem is through bottles and tubes of goo. We like to call it the *Highlander* school for young ladies. (There can be only one.) There's only space for one woman in the universe, so every woman's life goals depend on taking down every single other woman, with the eventual result that there will be exactly one surviving woman who will finally have earned the undivided attention of all men. Plus, she can finally get that job we all wanted to have, but couldn't because that company already had a woman.

Speaking of stupid ideas about women, here's one we've all heard at some point—that the route to success is not to be too awesome because that's intimidating, and no one will want you around. We like our women nice and mediocre, so that no one feels threatened by them. Is Amy Schumer unthreatening? Not fucking likely. But there's this ridiculous theory about how we prefer relatable (less meritorious) people around, which can be just a matter of perception. We can tear down Amy's looks to make her more "human" (in the sense above, the sense that doesn't mean "human" like a species of mammal but "human" like, look at that sack of shit running around the universe she's just as fucked up as I am definition of "human"), but that doesn't seem to make sense, because she's legit better at her discipline than a lot of other people, so maybe we should respect that. *No,* says the patriarchy, *if you admit she's a worthy human, that means you're not*. Admitting that any woman has ever been good in any respect seems threatening just because of our Highlander socialization process.

Freud had some interesting things to say about how we hate people who are most like us—people with the same name, who look like us, anyone to whom a meaningful comparison can be made. We think they're trying to steal our identity. They're going to take our place in the world, and off we'll go, still alive but with no purpose. There are quite a few movies about just that scenario. We shouldn't forget, though, that for women, that scenario is just co-existing with every other woman ever. That's why we have to compare Amy Schumer to every other female comedian, to see which one is the best, right? *There can be only one*. The losers are thrown into the center of the Earth.

The idea is that women are interchangeable. That's the whole idea of the patriarchy: that women have no individual characteristics and can therefore be easily replaced by any other woman. We have no special skills, no interesting thoughts to express, or even any physical characteristic that can be objectively valued above anyone else's such that we might claim the continued right to exist when other women also exist. We've all seen this formula in the movies. There is exactly one woman. All of the men are interested, but she's got her eye on the main character. Once they bang it out, it's done. She's taken care of as an existent and can safely retreat into the background of the hero's storyline, as long as she's fulfilled the role of being interesting enough—for a while—to make it believable that he'd be into her.

So it seems pretty important to be pretty—and by pretty, we mean nice to look at. And by nice to look at, we mean we need to embody any and every characteristic that every man has ever thought was pretty, or better yet, the exact one he currently thinks is pretty but soon won't, because there really is no such thing as objective beauty, and we're all just trying to keep up with the continuous flux of male opinion which, as we all know, is very important and unlike our opinions, can be expressed without thereby eliciting a comparison between the object of that opinion and the male who professes it. But then there's the other option: instead of trying to be pretty, we could just overthrow the patriarchy.

But that seems hard. So why not just be pretty? It is so unreasonable to just play along with the patriarchy, admit that women's self worth should be dependent on whether or not this bus driver thinks her perfume hides her human smell to the desired extent (but not enough to be whorish, of course). We could just choose to keep up with all of the latest fashion trends, read the women's magazines in order to figure out in which ways our spleen is ugly this month (and how to correct it before he notices!) and in general strive not only to *be* but to *feel* pretty, because those two things are definitely not the same.

Everyone thinks they get to have an opinion about "women," as if "women" is something up for debate, and everyone's opinion matters, so we can figure out what to do about the woman problem once and for all. It's not as though there were ever an opinion expressed about women by some bitter motherfucker or other that wasn't absolutely insightful. Women should just be everything men want, and then they would be happy—tall, but not too tall because that's emasculating, short; but not too short (who wants to look like they're dating a baby?); thin, but not too thin, because curves are sexy, except when they're fat, and for the love of God please never admit to the contortions you have to go through to look like that. And so on, and so on . . .

In addition to being entertaining, *I Feel Pretty* addresses some crucial feminist themes. A woman (played by Amy Schumer) has an accident in cycling class that entails some pretty fundamental changes to her life. Schumer's character doesn't end up paralyzed or maimed. The movie is a comedy. It's a story about self-discovery and triumph against all sorts of oppressive forces. Renee Bennett (played by Amy) hits her head, and wakes up thinking she is pretty.

The Oppressive Fashion-Beauty Complex

Way back in 1982—when most of us were young, carefree, and still thinking we were beautiful because a myriad of advertisements, magazine covers, billboards, TV shows, regrettable movies, and bullshit red-carpet interviews had not yet convinced us otherwise—Sandra Lee Bartky made the point that beauty standards, particularly as they are applied to women, are really a means of oppression.

We all want to be beautiful. We all want to feel pretty. There's nothing wrong with these feelings. The problem is that the desire to feel beautiful has been used by cosmetics manufacturers, marketing companies, and the fashion industry—a nefarious cabal that Bartky refers to as the "Fashion-Beauty Complex"—to make us buy shit. Bartky observes that, at least in the context of Western capitalism, in order to feel beautiful, we're told that we must smear our bodies with a myriad of creams, ointments, and goos, each designed to act against a different deficiency.

Are you growing old? Well you'd better use this super-duper anti-aging cream to get rid of those putatively heinous crow's feet. You're too pale? You should immediately part with your hard-earned cash to purchase this bronzing agent that will make you look like you spent countless summers on the sun-drenched beaches of the Mediterranean or some equally tropical locale. Once your skin is a slightly darker hue, you'd better run to the beauty counter at Bloomingdale's, Macy's, or Walgreens to pick up some ooze to make you look more like a ghost. Once you think you're done running around—and have come to the stomach-churning realization that you are ten steps closer to financial ruin—you find a moment's solace in the thought that you might have achieved the coveted status of being beautiful to Western eyes.

Then some washed-up actor and former cosmetics company spokesperson starts her own cosmetics line. Her face smiles at you from the covers of magazines at the supermarket counter. Your newsfeed is inundated with sponsored stories celebrating the miraculous properties of her beauty products every time you open your web-browser. With a sigh of resignation you reach for the last of your credit cards knowing that you'll max it out. At least you might feel pretty.

The sad reality is that we're being played. The Fashion-Beauty complex takes our desire to feel beautiful and commercializes it. The end result is than we're all smeared with goo, much less wealthy than we were at the start of our attempts to look like a million dollars.

All we have to do to understand how the Fashion-Beauty Complex oppresses women is to acknowledge that—in a capitalist system—the lack of financial prosperity amounts to lack of opportunity, and when opportunity is taken and we get nothing of significance in return that is oppression. The Fashion-Beauty Complex demands that we part with our money and promises that we will feel more beautiful. But we don't feel more beautiful, because the criteria of beauty are given by the very people that want us to buy the next thing that they manufacture.

The terrible truth of the Fashion-Beauty Complex is that it functions as a parasite that constantly offers us new things which we think will satiate our desire to feel beautiful, but no one thing offered by the Fashion-Beauty Complex actually succeeds in doing anything to make us feel more beautiful. We part with our money to buy the next putatively great product. Our servitude is measured in the amount of money we spend. We wanted to feel beautiful; we are made into slaves.

Amy Knows that Prettiness Is the Celebration of Your Difference

So what happens when you take a stand against your oppressors, are attacked, and then refuse to back down? W.E.B. Du Bois—who was no stranger to oppression—noticed that waging a battle against your oppressors tends to make you a bit fucked up, in the sense that you experience what he called "double consciousness." Essentially, you recognize that the world sees you one way—and treats you as one sort of thing—but, in fact you are aware that you're another sort of thing. An oppressed person experiences double consciousness when they are simultaneously aware of what the world thinks they are *and* they are also aware that they are something radically different from that thing that the oppressor thinks that they are.

One idea about how to right the wrongs of the oppressive reality that women have to live with every day—a reality which involves concepts of beauty as a means of oppression—came from John Rawls's massive *Theory of Justice*. Rawls is a guy who was hugely influential, even though he never tried to change his whole life after a peloton accident. The central claim of Rawls's theory is that we can get rid of oppression if we give people what they deserve. It seems like a pretty damn good theory, in the sense that it doesn't seem that anybody could really claim that they are slaves, hard-done-by, or otherwise wronged, if they are getting a fair share of the things that everyone else has. Rawls made his philosophical career by claiming that justice is essentially having the same access to stuff that everyone else has. Imagine you're in a society that values shiny doom-a-fliggies. Everybody likes these things. If you have the doom-a-fliggies that you deserve, then you're living in a just society. For Rawls, you can't make the case that you are oppressed if you have the right amount of doom-a-fliggies. The fundamental question is: Can we make a society that distributes the doom-a-fliggies in a fair way? If we can, then we are awesome. If we can't, then we suck and we live in an oppressive society.

As a pretty privileged white guy who got his degrees from some of the nation's elite educational institutions, Rawls probably never gave much thought to whether or not he felt pretty—or how he might need to modify his body to feel pretty. Despite all his privilege, he was willing to grant that there was a period in recent American history in which women—and various other minorities—might have legitimately felt oppressed. But for Rawls, those times are—for the most part—gone. As a society, we have re-jiggered our distribution of things so everybody—regardless of their gender—can get the fair amount of stuff.

Take a look around. If society is so fair, then why the hell doesn't it seem that fair at all? It doesn't seem like everybody is all kumbaya, holding hands, getting exactly what they should get. And even if people are getting all the physical stuff they need—even if there's no material privation—that doesn't mean that there is no oppression going on. Just because you can go to a movie theater—hopefully to see an awesome Amy Schumer movie—and have a choice between forty-seven different flavor combinations of soda pop, any one of which costs the same as the other, this doesn't mean that there you aren't oppressed. The distribution of things, and the supposedly equal opportunity to get stuff, doesn't mean that you aren't an oppressed person. Ask that person at the movie theater who spent a boatload of cash, and a whole bunch of time trying to look pretty, if she feels totally liberated. News flash: she doesn't.

In *Justice and the Politics of Difference* (which is one of the most important—and readable—books of feminist philosophy ever published) Iris Marion Young takes Rawls to task. Young points out that we feel oppressed when we don't have the same rights as another person, and whatever rights are they are not the sort of things that can be handed-out like popcorn or soda pop. Rights are concepts about how we should govern ourselves, they are rules. Rights are not material things that can be distributed. Rawls conceived of rights as being analogous to material things, and, on the basis of this analogy he thought societies could distribute rights just like we can distribute material things. The problem is that we can't. Rights are not like physical things. Rawls attempted to solve the problem of oppression by thinking of rights as distributable things. His solution to oppression doesn't work because he provided an answer based on a wonky concept of what rights are.

Though Young's point that all distributive justice is based on a stupid concept of what rights are is a definitive argument against Rawls' entire theory, Young was just getting started. Young's second argument against Rawls is that his entire theory of justice comes from a position of privilege and tends to enforce that privilege. It's easy to say that your beauty doesn't matter, when you have been told for your entire life that you are beautiful, and now you make your money as a super-model.

Rawls's key idea is that we can have a fair—that is non-oppressive—society if we just imagine ourselves as the same as everybody else, and then ask what sorts of rights and freedoms would we want. This sort of imaginary step basically asks us to eliminate any concept we might have of our difference from anyone else. If we think of ourselves as being the same as everyone else, then we'll get rid of all prejudice.

If we think everyone's the same, then no-one will feel oppressed. Does that seem right to you? Young thought it was bullshit. You know who thinks of all people as the same? A guy who is pretty damn comfortable with who he is and thinks that everybody should basically be like him. It's really easy to think that everybody should get rid of any concept of difference when you have never been marginalized, derided, mocked, oppressed and kicked around because you were different. Young says that the idea that everybody should think of themselves as the same—the fundamental claim of Rawls' theory—really amounts to saying that everybody should be like the person making the claim. This theory doesn't get rid of oppression, it makes things more oppressive.

For Young, one of the best ways to get rid of oppression is to stop listening to what all the privileged—that is white males—have to say. What oppressed people need to do is start speaking up, and celebrating their differences from everyone else. And this is exactly what Amy Schumer is doing. In making an awesome movie about how she is pretty, Amy is demonstrating how the oppressive standards of beauty are bullshit. Amy is saying that prettiness is the celebration of who you are, the celebration of what you are.

19
How to Feel Pretty

THE PATRIARCHY

Listen up, bitches.

There's been a lot of talk lately about women. Are they people? Are they a *kind* of people? Not if that means I can't own them, like I do animals. So no, because we all know that "woman" the opposite of "man," which we all know is short for "human." Therefore women are not humans. Still, should we be nice and allow them do people things, or will that lead to the end of civil society? People keep saying crazy things like that women should control their own bodies. They say that women deserve equal pay for inferior work, and that you should just let these psychos ruin people's lives, running around telling lies about being sexually assaulted. I mean, we've all made bad decisions before, but I'm not about to threaten someone's career over it. Sex is fun, right? I'm not even sure you *can* force someone into doing something fun. I mean, women should be a little more grateful for everything we've let them get away with so far—maybe they shouldn't push their luck. Save some of the human things for the real people—men.

Of course, I am very understanding (my Mom said so), and I know that there are some things about themselves that women cannot change—like not being worthy of a man's salary, not being able to control their emotions, abstract thought in general. While all of this is women's fault, and they should definitely still feel badly about it, they should also still feel grateful that I'm willing to allow this to continue. But then there are the things you can change, even with the diminished capacities of a woman.

Now women, I'm not trying to tell you what to do. That would be sexist. But, really, if your life is ever going to have any meaning, you should probably go find a man before your ovaries shrivel up and you become useless. And to do that, you need to feel pretty. Feeling pretty isn't just saying to yourself, "Oh, my physical form is sufficiently attractive." It's about internalizing the demands of patriarchal society and using them as the sole measure according to which you might judge your success as a woman. I know that sounds complicated, but don't worry—I'm here to help.

Because apparently you're too busy sobbing about your periods to go read a magazine, here's an overview of everything you've missed. These are some tried and true methods for how to revive your self esteem in face of the fact that you're garbage and nobody loves you. Now this may sound like tough love, but you bitches have gone a little off-track, forgetting that it's your biological imperative to breed sacks full of babies, only half of which turn out to be people anyway. Well I'm sick of humoring you. Why is it always the ugly bitches who call themselves feminists? Maybe if they knew *how* to be pretty, they'd be able to keep a man, and then they wouldn't have so much free time to run around whining. So here's your new guide to life, Feminazis—and remember, this is for your own good, and trust me, I know what's good for you, Sweetie. Because I'm smart.

How to Feel Pretty #1: Your Face

Your face is bullshit. I can see exactly where the flesh parts are on it, and I'm judging them. You should probably just hide in a closet, but I think that's weak, and I don't like weak women. So get the fuck out so I can make a face at your face to indicate how displeased I am with it.

First of all, there are holes all over the place. The ones in your skin are probably too big, and the ones in your nose, too, but your eye holes and mouth holes might be too small, unless they aren't today. You should try hiding most of your face with paint, to start. It should appear almost flesh-like, but without any of the human-y bits of flesh. It should be smooth but not too smooth. Try painting over it in a solid flesh tone and then painting over that to reintroduce lines mimicking the bone structure that I have decided is in fashion this month. (Don't worry, your particular bone structure will never be in fashion, because it sucks.)

Maybe your ears are sticking out too much and I don't feel like it's cute today. Tape that shit down. Add some shiny things to the rims so that I don't have to look directly at them. Your eyebrows are all over the place and not the right color for your face. This one time, I saw a girl with an eyebrow ring, and I thought that was hot, but not on you. Take it out and if it scars, I'm going to remark on it forever, about how you ruined your face. Your eyes should be whatever color I decide is most soulful, and you should accentuate that with the appropriate lines drawn around them and some crap on those tiny hairs. Sometimes, I'm just sick of your face, and I wish you were a redhead. You could be, you know. You're just not trying.

It would be nice if you just didn't have a face, because then you could draw on whatever one occurred to me as being the best at any given time. Sometimes I'm into Peggy from *Mad Men*, but other times, she's in *The Handmaid's Tale*, and feminists are always ugly and that's why they can't keep a man unless they emasculate them with their book learning and refuse to bear their children. I don't want a blank face, though, because I like a face with personality—that's a term I use to make you think that whatever I'm talking about isn't pretty. It's *charming* that your lips are too thin; I'll let it slide as long as you recognize how nice I'm being about it.

Once you've got that whole face over your face, you should remember that it's still only going to look good in certain lighting and only in comparison to some other parts of the universe. You should avoid bright sunshine, because I can find wrinkles on a baby and rest assured, whatever inner beauty you have is fleeting. You should practice making faces in the mirror before you go out in public—ever. Some facial muscles just weren't meant to be used. They should atrophy and die, as you wrangle your ugly paint face into only the most flattering expressions. Try laughing. Wasn't that gross? You're fucking ugly. Try laughing like a lady. Sometimes, though, it's nice to be around someone who laughs boisterously and doesn't care what their face looks like. It would be weird if you did it, though.

Your picture face should always be ready to go. Don't worry if you don't look like your picture face in real life. People would rather stare at an attractive picture than recognize that you're a real person, any day. Just go with it, and make sure it comes off as natural. While you're at it, make sure that any pictures of you that do make it out have your choice of filter and have been run through that app that makes another face on top of your makeup face. Your makeup can't hide the fact that there's flesh back there, but the app can. You should be cartoonishly smooth, with white teeth, big hair, and absolutely no eye veins. Thin out that chin a little bit, make sure your face still matches your neck, and you could still feel pretty, I guess. Everyone will be able to tell it's not natural, though, so probably not.

How to Feel Pretty #2: Your Hair

Short hair is unfeminine, and long hair takes too long to deal with. You should have both. You were probably born with the wrong color of hair for your skin tone, and even if you weren't, your current hair color isn't in style at the moment, by which I mean it should look like that waitress character on television whose boobs I like, but also you should be her and not you. Your hair should always appear as if no effort has gone into it, but if it strays from the exact position that makes your forehead not look ridiculous, I'm going to notice. So maybe try one of those firm fix products and then before you let anyone touch it, wash and dry your hair so that it doesn't feel like stickers. Of course, this means you can only let people either see or touch your hair at one time—never both. That would ruin the illusion.

Short hair is very in fashion, if your hairstyle is *for you*, which is also in fashion. But it's not the kind of fashion that's going to stop people from saying, "She's given up." I mean, it's cute and all, but not all the time. Now you just look like someone who doesn't want to do their hair every day. Don't you care what people think of you?

Long hair is a good standby. If your hair is straight, curl it. If it's curly, straighten it. You could get bangs, if you want to look like someone just coming out of a long relationship that ended badly. Without bangs, it's kind of boring, though, just boring old long hair that takes too long to wash and dry and curl and straighten and affix properly.

Speaking of which, you're taking much too long already. Couldn't you just have a face made of paint and hair that is naturally voluminous, tamed, and colored whatever the color of the month is but most importantly, not at all damaged? (Because I hate when women look "fake.") That seems easier; you should try it. Maybe you could get away with a ponytail sometimes, if I've recently seen some other woman with a ponytail I thought was attractive and could transfer that association over to you.

Your hair is too thin, and you should get extensions. That shouldn't interfere with shower sex, though, and I'd still like to be able to spontaneously push you into a pool if I'm in a whimsical mood and see you rise up from said pool looking like Denise Richards in *Wild Things*. If I can't do that, I'm going to say that you care about your appearance way too much, and that you're so fucking vain—shallow, even. I really don't care about your appearance, as long as it meets my ludicrous standards at all times.

How to Feel Pretty #3: Your Body

I care more about the appearance of your body than you'll ever know. Every mole is a sign of skin cancer that I don't want to pass on to my children, which I assume you'll be caring for if I decide you worthy. Maybe if it's just one mole in just the right spot, but not like, anything permanent. You're too fat and too thin—basically, your proportions are all wrong *and* if they weren't, you'd still be the wrong size. I like a woman I can grab on to, whose ribs I can see clearly from across the room, who's athletic enough to keep up with my own prowess but not *manly*, which (like a lot of words) is a word I'm going to use whenever I want you to feel bad and therefore be more likely to sleep with me because I think you're totally hot, you ugly bitch.

"Milk, Milk, Lemonade" is at once both a reminder that women are people, but also a showcase for butts, and I therefore find it both alluring and disgusting. You should work that out somehow, you know, from a woman's perspective (which I value to the extent that it's my perspective, but spoken in a higher tone).

I don't think I have to even mention that you should be smaller than you are. It's not that I want to imagine you not being able to leave home because of a particularly rough cleanse, during which you think your insides might end up outside, but I'd still like to see how that turns out—as long as it's not going to ruin my weekend, because I was kind of hoping you could schedule your disgusting beauty regimen around when I think you should be available, which is whenever. (Don't get all uptight about it; the fact that I'm spontaneous means you have to be available for that, *all the time*. Keep those rollers in, girly, cause I could show up whenever, and you'd better be ready to take them out during the amount of time I think it takes to walk from the far end of your apartment to the front door.)

You should show enough of your body to keep me interested, but if I see it, I'll either not be interested, because there's no mystery anymore, or I'll be super-interested and assholes on the Internet will blame you if you end up raped. I'm confident enough in myself to assert that you're only wearing lipstick to get my attention, but if you don't wear it, it's because you're a slob who doesn't care about your appearance—and that's so unprofessional. No wonder we keep hiring men. At least they can walk around without looking like slobs or sluts. But I'm getting sidetracked here.

Ideally, your body should take up no space but also appear to me as an apparition, having no human functionality whatsoever but, you know, in a way that seems *real,* because I hate fake bitches.

How to Feel Pretty #4: Just Go Bang Everyone

As long as you don't go bang everyone like a *whore* would, it's fine. You can finally get away from the bathroom mirror and out into the real world, where at random moments you'll realize that it doesn't matter whether your new eyelashes are real horsehair because you can always catch a dick (just like Amy in NYC). It's almost as if those ridiculous beauty standards are there *just* to make women feel bad, but that can't be true, because they're going to make you feel pretty, and pretty is good, right? It's almost like it doesn't fucking matter what you look like, because out in the universe, people are always fucking other people, and babies keep being made despite the fact that you're factoring that volumizer into next month's budget and not this one.

How to Feel Pretty #5: Don't Just Go Bang Everyone

You're only doing that because your self-esteem is bad, and that's another thing you should feel badly about. The world is full of assholes, and you don't want to bang them anyway. You should just go dress yourself up and feel pretty and then not let anyone ruin that for you, except for that one guy who's so nice, but also all of the other nice guys, because they all have earned you in some way, but not like, *all* of them, because every one of them is unique and special and deserving of your affections, which means you have to be faithful to them—all of them.

How to Feel Pretty #6: Focus on Your Own Accomplishments

Maybe you don't need anyone else to be happy. Maybe you can be satisfied with accomplishing great things in life and not worry about interpersonal relationships. Wouldn't that be nice? That's what you'll need to think, at least, because accomplishments themselves are unattractive. You don't want to have too many of them, because men hate smart women, unless it's for the sake of telling people how smart their woman is, which makes them smarter. Also, your accomplishments are stupid, and I don't know how you expect anyone to take them seriously when your eyebrows are so out of whack. Maybe you should try being friendlier; networking is an important part of working your way up the corporate ladder, but we're still promoting Jim because, sure, people like to be around you because you're *nice*, but we don't really think you can *cut it* as an executive. We're looking for someone with *merit*, not just social skills. You can try to smile, in which case I'm going to think you're ineffective, or you can not, in which case you should realize that your attitude is affecting your job performance, and that's going in your annual report. You can still plan the Xmas party, though, and I'm sure Jim would appreciate it, because he's about to be very busy.

It's just that I like women who have their own interests and goals—as long as they're attractive ones and they don't interfere with my plans for how you'll support my own accomplishments in life. Maybe you could model on the weekends and make enough money to support us both, so that I can play the guitar while you find that very attractive.

How to Feel Pretty #7: Go Ahead and Die

You're not getting any younger, it's going to happen anyway, and I'd prefer to mourn you occasionally in my thoughts as I finger-bang multitudes of other women, each of whom I don't have to treat as a human because they're mere flesh replacements for my idealized version of a woman who never existed but who was polite enough to *die* and therefore not ruin my illusion. Try to make it pretty, too. I don't want to see any intestines in a car accident, or something. Perhaps use a poison that freezes your face into an expression of your longing for me as the light fades from your eyes. The mortician has really good cover-up. (See again, How to Feel Pretty #1.)

Now that that's clear, I don't want to hear anything else about how you "deserve" better. Just follow these simple guidelines, and maybe you'll actually convince me you're worth being treated like a human. After all, I believe in equality.

References

Aristotle. 1999. *Nicomachean Ethics*. Hackett.

Balsam, Kimberly F., and Dawn M. Szymanski. 2005. Relationship Quality and Domestic Violence in Women's Same-Sex Relationships: The Role of Minority Stress. *Psychology of Women Quarterly* 29:3.

Bandura, Albert. 1997. *Self-Efficacy: The Exercise of Control*. Freeman.

Beauvoir, Simone de. 2011 [1949]. *The Second Sex*. Random House.

Bettcher, Talia Mae. 2006. Appearance, Reality, and Gender Deception: Reflections on Transphobic Violence and the Politics of Pretence. In Felix Ó Murchadha, ed., *Violence, Victims, Justifications: Philosophical Approaches*. Peter Lang.

Brownmiller, Susan. 2013. *Against Our Will: Men, Women, and Rape*. Open Road Media.

Bruenig, Elizabeth. 2015. Comedians Are Funny, Not Public Intellectuals. *The New Republic* (June 3rd).

Carroll, Noël. 2014. *Humour: A Very Short Introduction*. Oxford University Press.

———. 2017. Timings. Keynote Address at the Ethics and Aesthetics of Stand-Up Comedy Conference <www.youtube.com/watch?v=St45CpF-rDc>.

Centers for Disease Control and Prevention. 2017. *Sex Offenses and Offenders: An Analysis of Data on Rape and Sexual Assault*.

Cixous, Hélène. 1976. The Laugh of the Medusa. *Signs* 1:4.

Cudd, Ann E. 2006. *Analyzing Oppression*. Oxford University Press.

Debord, Guy. 1994 [1967]. *The Society of the Spectacle*. Cambridge University Press.

———. 1998 [1988]. *Comments on the Society of the Spectacle*. Verso.

Donovan, Sarah K. n.d. Luce Irigaray (1932?–). *Internet Encyclopedia of Philosophy*.

Foucault, Michel. 1976. *The History of Sexuality*. Pantheon.

Freud, Sigmund S. 1920. *Wit and Its Relation to the Unconscious*. Kegan Paul.

Fricker, Miranda. 2007. *Epistemic Injustice: Power and the Ethics of Knowing*. Oxford University Press.

Garber, Megan. 2015. How Comedians Became Public Intellectuals. *The Atlantic* (May 28th).

Gray, Frances. 1994. *Women and Laughter*. University Press of Virginia.

Hume, David. 1910 [1757]. Of the Standard of Taste. In C.W. Eliott, ed., *English Essays from Sir Philip Sidney to Macaulay*. Collier.

Irigaray, Luce. 1985. *Speculum of the Other Woman*. Cornell University Press.

Kahneman, Daniel. 2011. *Thinking, Fast and Slow*. Farrar, Straus, and Giroux.

Kim, Jane. 2012. Taking Rape Seriously: Rape as Slavery. *Harvard Journal of Law and Gender* 35.

Mercer, Mark. 1998. Psychological Egoism and Its Critics. *Southern Journal of Philosophy* 36.

Möller, Anna, Hans Peter Sondergaard, and Loti Helström. 2017. Tonic Immobility during Sexual Assault: A Common Reaction Predicting Posttraumatic Stress Disorder and Severe Depression. *Acta Obstetrica et Gynecologica Scandinavica* 96:8 (June).

Nietzsche, Friedrich. 1985. *Thus Spoke Zarathustra: A Book for Everyone and No One*. Penguin.

———. 2001. *The Gay Science*. Cambridge University Press.

———. 2009. *On the Genealogy of Morals*. Oxford University Press.

Nussbaum, Emily. 2015. The Little Tramp: The Raucous Feminist Humor of "Inside Amy Schumer." *The New Yorker* (May 11th).

Paul, Ellen, Fred D. Miller, and Jeffrey Paul, eds. 1997. *Self-Interest*. Cambridge University Press.

Plato. 1997. *Complete Works*. Hackett.

Rorty, Richard. 1989. *Contingency, Irony, and Solidarity*. Cambridge University Press.

Sepinwall, Alan. 2015. Amy Schumer on Her "12 Angry Men" Spoof: I'm More Proud of It than Anything I've Ever Done. *Uproxx* (May 5th).

Wilson, David Sloan. *Does Altruism Exist? Culture, Genes, and the Welfare of Others* (New Haven: Yale University Press, 2015).

Author Bios

Robert Arp, PhD, has interests in several areas of philosophy. He thinks that "Girl, You Don't Need Makeup" is actually a neo-feminist re-imagining of a deconstructionist take on nihilistic existentialism's final cry for respite in a forgotten American culture rife with undertones of totalitarianism, but still retaining overtones of a former egalitarian proletariat. Oh, and he also agrees with the boy band that the bitch definitely needs makeup.

Camille Atkinson earned a PhD in philosophy from the New School for Social Research. Since then, she has traveled extensively—both literally and metaphorically. Recently, she allowed Schumer's humor to take her into the most dangerous neighborhoods of her own mental landscape and, with beloved canines in tow, crisscrossed the continental United States. She is currently in Texas, where she's faced the challenges of teaching in prison and adapting to small town living.

Gregor Balke, PhD, has written essays on some of his favorite things on TV, including *Seinfeld*, *30 Rock*, *Curb Your Enthusiasm*, and sitcoms in general. He saw Amy Schumer once at her show in Oslo, while she was on her European Tour in 2016. Since then, he is looking for more things they have in common other than that they were in the same room that night. So far, he has been able to determine their common preference for drinks, humor (obviously), and the fact that they share the same year of birth.

Gerald Browning spends his time teaching students how to write gooder as adjunct faculty of English at Muskegon Community College. When he isn't in the classroom, he's spending his extra time with his family or cross-training in martial arts (probably to overcompensate for something).

Noël Carroll is Distinguished Professor of Philosophy at the Graduate Center of the City University, where he's planning a course entitled "Classic Texts in the Philosophy of Love: Schumer, Silverman, and Diotima."

Michelle Ciurria is a visiting scholar at the University of Missouri–St. Louis. Her main research interest is responsibility. Between re-watching episodes of *Inside Amy Schumer*, looking at pictures of cats on Pinterest, and searching the Web for creative pizza recipes, she barely managed to submit her manuscript for this edited volume on time. It's a work in progress!

Verena Ehrnberger is currently working as a legal expert and studies philosophy and psychotherapy in Vienna. What amazes her the most about Amy Schumer's comedy is that it encompasses all of her favorite things: challenging the status quo, asking the tough questions and righting societal wrongs by pointing them out. Also, she does have a lower back tattoo. (All adventurous women do.)

Charlene Elsby, PhD, is Assistant Professor and the Philosophy Program Director at Purdue Fort Wayne, researching Aristotle and realist phenomenology. Once this book comes out, though, she plans to give up the glamorous life of an academic, because Amy Schumer will realize how hilarious she is and personally recruit her as a writer for her *Inside Amy Schumer* and other projects, despite having general concerns over whether Elsby's love for Schumer borders on the inappropriate. (And when we say "borders on," we mean "definitely crosses a line.")

Karen Flieswasser left the ivory tower a while ago, but couldn't resist writing a chapter on pop culture and philosophy. She holds a Bachelor of Arts in Philosophy from KU Leuven and a Master of Science in Philosophy of Science from the London School of Economics and Political Science.

JERED JANES almost never writes about himself in the third person. When he does, it usually goes something like this: Jered is a PhD candidate in philosophy at Marquette University, where he works on issues in phenomenology, philosophy of mind, and philosophical pedagogy. He thinks comedians provide audiences with unique and excellent opportunities to think about philosophical issues, and he isn't joking.

LEIGH KOLB teaches English and Journalism at East Central College in Missouri. She's contributed to *Sons of Anarchy and Philosophy*, *Philosophy and Breaking Bad*, and *Twin Peaks and Philosophy*, and written for *Vulture* and *Bitch* Magazine. She's thankful that the universe assures her that she's perfect, no matter how she acts.

CECILIA LI is completing her PhD in Philosophy at the University of Western Ontario. When she is not busy writing her dissertation on Plato's theory of craft knowledge, she enjoys contemplating the Forms, drinking out of giant wine glasses and ordering pastitzza at 3:00 A.M.

ROB LUZECKY is a lecturer in philosophy at Purdue Fort Wayne, where he corrupts the youth with artworks on the theory that beauty and moral rectitude are not equivalent terms. He thinks Amy Schumer is fucking hilarious, and there's nothing wrong with that.

DANIEL MALLOY teaches philosophy at Aims Community College in Greeley, Colorado. He . . . I mean, really . . . he . . . I'm not drunk! You're drunk! *hic* . . . what was I saying? . . . *burp* . . . Yeah! He's . . . okay, okay, okay . . . He's like, this guy . . . something, something *mumble* . . . I'm okay, 'm okay . . . *thump!* zzzzzzzz . . .

FERNANDO GABRIEL PAGNONI BERNS is a PhD student and also a professor at Universidad de Buenos Aires (UBA), Facultad de Filosofía y Letras (Argentina). He discovered Amy Schumer only after reading an Open Court call for papers requesting abstracts for a book about this woman. Intrigued about who she was and why she deserved a book, he saw her show . . . and loved it. Soon, he was scribbling the abstract, and here is the final result. So, thanks, Open Court, for publishing the chapter and pointing him in Amy's direction.

JENNIFER WARE is a doctoral candidate in the Philosophy Department at the City University of New York, Graduate Center. Her research interests include humor, derogatory language, and feminism, so this book seemed like a good match. Like Amy Schumer, Jennifer has a degree in theater, enjoys white wine, and is best friends with her sister. (Hi, Ariel!)

Index